A Chef's Companion to Cost Control

Resource information for financially responsible Chefs, Cooks and Managers

Klaus Theyer CCC

KENDALL/HUNT PUBLISHING COMPANY
4050 Westmark Drive　　　Dubuque, Iowa 52002

Foreword

This publication was prepared after years of frustration searching for a quick reference referring to terminology, formulas and examples of Costing Applications in the Hospitality Industry.

I have read many publications on this topic, used some of them for teaching this topic to students, aspiring managers and cooks alike (chefs are cooks too) without finding one with the right mix of essential information and examples. It appears that the majority of these publications were written for middle management who deal with theoretical cost control on a daily basis, leaving occasional users in need of a quick reference without a resource for their needs.

In this publication I aim to explain cost, identification, principles, formulas and their intended application, as well as basic control methods in a manner anyone should be able to use.

This publication does not intend to cover accounting principles or methods. Readers are encouraged to seek competent professional advice and services.

After reading and using this publication, please let me know if I have achieved my goal. If you have any suggestions for improving this publication or on topics you think should be covered, do not hesitate to contact me and share your thoughts.

For updates, corrections and communication, please visit my website *www.MenuForProfit.com* Your comments are welcome and appreciated.

Klaus Theyer CCC

Credits:
Proofreading: Ann Formella
Book cover design: Pat Cuda
Photo credits: Sara Martins (*sara.s.martins@hotmail.com*)

Copyright © 2005, 2007 by Klaus Theyer

ISBN 978-0-7575-4762-1

Kendall/Hunt Publishing Company has the exclusive rights to reproduce this work,
to prepare derivative works from this work, to publicly distribute this work,
to publicly perform this work and to publicly display this work.

All rights reserved. No part of this publication may be reproduced,
stored in a retrieval system, or transmitted, in any form or by any
means, electronic, mechanical, photocopying, recording, or otherwise,
without the prior written permission of the copyright owner.

Printed in the United States of America
10 9 8 7 6 5 4 3 2 1

CONTENTS   **Page #**

Basic Income statement structure   6
Break-Even-Point   65 - 68
Budget – Financial Forecast – Projection – The Operations Budget   43 - 50
Budget, Sales, Variance Report   77
Calculation of Menu Item Cost   28
Canadian payroll – mandatory deductions (January2007)   24 - 27
COGS Cost of Goods Sold   19 - 21
Cost Classification   5
Cost consideration, Costs and Selling Price calculations, Ideal Cost   12 - 24
Cost Control terminology vs. Accounting terminology   4
Cost, Cost%, Selling price, Profit Margin, Popularity   7 - 18
Definition of Unit, Unit Cost and Line Cost   35 - 36
Definition, Terminology, Abbreviation, Acronyms explained   2 - 3
Depreciation – Capital Cost Allowance   82 - 84
Example of Cost allocation with Prime Cost   8
Extended COGS Calculation   20 - 21
Introduction   1
Inventory, Inventory Costing - Dill Pickles example   58 - 64
Labour - Staff cost - Canadian payroll   23 - 27
Let's Sell - Selling Price calculations   34 - 36
Line Cost Sample   36
Menu Analysis – Menu Engineering   69 - 81
Menu Item Cost Consideration   28
Product Inventory extended cost calculations   59 - 64
Purchasing, Receiving, Storing - simplified   51 - 59
Sales Mix example   76
Sales to Cost relation and examples   30 - 31
Simplified Restaurant – Hotel Revenue and Cost Areas   10 - 11
Standard Recipe and Forms   28 - 34, 101 & 103
Yield Calculations   37 - 42

Templates and Workshops   86

Quick Conversions – Recipe Conversions   87 - 88
Calculator Warm-up   89 - 90
Easy Workshop   91 - 92
Yield Test "A"   93 - 94
Bar Inventory   95 - 96
Menu Analysis "Bar One"   97 - 98
Turkey Yield   99 - 100
Standard Recipe "Singapore Sling"   101
Simple Menu Analysis   102
Standard Recipe "Vichyssoise"   103
Sales/Cost/Cost%/Yield/Loss Formulae   104
The Percentage Pie   105
From ONE dollar to a GOOGOLPLEX   106

Introduction

**The intend of this publication is to assist you in understanding what COST is, how it occurs, how the term is used, to recognise that in different situations it may mean different things and that it needs to be monitored and controlled.
Cost communicated properly may help cooks to understand managements goals and objectives and chefs/managers to manage more effectively.**

The word Cost, by itself, is often referred to or quoted in many situations and equally often misinterpreted, or not fully understood.

In accounting terms, Cost is a REDUCTION IN VALUE OF AN ASSET (something the company owns) for the PURPOSE OF SECURING BENEFIT OR GAIN (Sales, Profit). Cost in accounting terms is most often referred to as Expense, which is true most of the time, unless it refers, directly or indirectly, to Cost of Goods Sold or for Sale, in which case other factors need to be considered.

Let me provide you a few examples:
When you pay a Mortgage or Rent, Property taxes, Insurance and other Expenses, which you have to pay if the business is operating or closed, such Expenses are referred to as **Fixed Cost (Occupancy Cost)**. These Fixed Cost occur every day (being used up) and are Costs which are not likely to change in a short period of time. This type of Cost, in most cases also include Labour Cost. Labour must be on the premises in order to operate – even if there are no customers coming through the door.

When fixtures and equipment are being purchased, the Cost incurring to the business, although it is a Cost, is also an investment which establishes, or increases, the value of the business and therefore is recorded as an **Asset** in Financial Statements (Balance Sheet). Assets fall into two major groups: Fixed Assets (Long term and sometimes depreciable) which are not intended to be sold, and Liquid Assets (Short term) which can easily be converted into Cash, such as Cash itself, Cheques, Credit card payments and products for Sale (Food and Beverage). The saleable **Assets** are referred to as **Inventory** for Sale.

At this point, although money may has been laid out to acquire these goods, no Cost has occurred, since all these Goods are still available for Sale.

This situation changes when product is no longer available for sale due to spoilage, breaks, expiry or theft. The value of the product which is lost (no longer available for sale) has now changed from an investment (Asset-Inventory) to an Expense or Cost.

The situation also changes when product is removed from Inventory to be prepared for sale and is subsequently sold (a meal or a drink) it is then referred to as **Cost of Goods Sold**, or abbreviated as **COGS**.

Definitions, Terminology	Abbreviation	Explanation if necessary
Actual Cost %	ACT %	Calculated based on COGS and Revenue
Adjusted	ADJ	Projected +/- Variance
Alternative Cost	ALTC	Term used for Profit in Cost Control
As Purchased	AP	Considered to be 100%
Average and/or mean	AVG	For a data set, the mean is the sum of the observations divided by the number of observations
Average Contribution Margin	ACM	ACM = (AVS – AVC)
Average Sales	AVS	Sales divided by # of customers
Average Variable Cost	AVC	AVC = (VA div. # Customers)
Average Variable Rate	AVR	Ratio of AVC to AVS (decimal)
Break Even Point	BEP	When Revenue covers all Costs
Budget (Long term or Short term, Static or Flexible)	Budget	Financial Forecast, usually based on Historical information, most often for Sales and Costs
Capital Cost	CC	Cost of Capital investment
Capital Cost Allowance	CCA	Determined by Class # and percentage, reduction of Income by claiming the Value of Loss over Time from Assets.
Closing Inventory	C I	The Value of Inventory at end of (Time/Date)
Contribution Margin	C M	CM = (S – VC)
Contribution Rate	C R	CR = (1 – VR)
Cost of Goods Sold	DVC	Directly Variable Cost – Product used for Sales
Depreciation	Dep	Loss of Value over time – offset by CCA
Desired or Planned or Target or Budgeted or Forecasted or Standard or Ideal Cost %	DC %	Percentage used to calculate potential Selling Prices
Edible Portion	E P	Final Consumable Product (See Yield)
Fixed Cost	FXC or OH	Overhead Cost - Occupancy Cost
Gross Profit	G P	CM, Contribution towards Profit
Historical Cost		Budgetary Term for Cost in the past
Indirect Costs		Variable Cost – Anticipated Sales surrounding cost
Loss	L	Difference between AP and EP
Menu Mix or Sales Mix or Popularity Index (%)	MM or SM or PI	Item sold divided by total items sold, usually expressed as %
Net Income	Net	Accounting expression for Profit
Opening Inventory	O I	The Value of Inventory at the beginning of (Time/Date) usually closing inventory from previous period.
Overhead Cost – Occupancy Cost	FXC or OH	Fixed Cost occurring with or without a Sale
Planned Cost	See DC %	Historical or other Cost information applied

Point of Sales	POS	Cash register, Computer terminal recording orders and sales
Prime Cost	PC	Combined Cost of Product and Labour
Profit Margin	PM	Difference between Revenue and Costs
Profit or Alternative Cost	P	Another word for Net Income
Projected Cost Percentage	PC %	Based on anticipated Sales mix
Proportional Share of Total Sales (Revenue)	PSTS	Ratio of one (type) Unit Sale to total Units Sold
Purchase	P	Abbreviation used in COGS calculation
Purchase Order	P.O.	External requisition for selected Vendor
Purchase Order Number	P.O. #	A unique number for each P.O. issued
Ratio	Ratio	A method of evaluating comparables.
Revenue	REV	Accrued Sales (Income)
Sale(s)	S	Earnings in exchange for Goods sold or Services rendered
Semi-Variable Cost (FXC and VC)	SVC	Labour Cost (however, most often calculated as part of FXC)
Unit, or Recipe Unit	Unit - RU	Smallest dividable amount of quantity, or predetermined quantity
Unit Sales Required to Break Even	USRB	See Break Even Point USRB = (FXC per Unit div. CM per Unit)
Usable Portion	UP	Trimmed/Boned, prior to cooking
Variable Cost	VC	Sales surrounding Cost
Variable Rate	VR	VR = (VC div. by S) usually expressed as fraction
Variance	VAR	Difference between Desired/Projected and Actual
Zero Based Budget	ZBB	In simple terms, ZBB does not consider Historical cost. Budget items must be defended.

Space for your own abbreviations and acronyms.

Cost Control terminology vs. Accounting terminology

I am using an Income Statement format, the official name for it is: "Statement of Income and Expenses", which is also commonly used as a template for a "Budget" to demonstrate the difference between the terms used in Accounting and Cost Control.

Accounting terms:	Cost Control terms:
INCOME:	**INCOME:**
Sales, Revenue (Accrued Sales)	Sales, Revenue (Accrued Sales)
Cost of Sale Material Cost (Cost of good or COGS)	**Cost of Goods Sold** (COGS) the actual cost of products being sold (Directly Variable Cost **DVC**)
Gross Profit or Profit Margin:	**Gross Profit or Contribution Margin:**
EXPENSES:	**COSTS:**
Operational Expenses: Sales related expenses, Advertising and Promotions	**Variable Cost** (in relation to Sales) This Cost is an indirect cost, occurring because of a sale being anticipated or made, i.e. Condiments,
FIXED Expenses: Overhead (Rent, Insurance (Labour))	**FIXED Cost: (FXC)** (Occupancy Cost) Overhead (Rent, Insurance, (Labour))
Labour Expense including Benefits	Labour Cost **(SVC)** Semi-Variable Cost – Note: Most establishments handle Labour Cost as a Fixed Cost
Net Income (Loss):	**Profit (Loss)** Alternative Cost **(ALTC)**

NOTE: **Fixed Cost** can be defined as: Cost/Expense occurring without or with a Sale being made.

Accrued means accumulated – Sales become Revenue when measured for a period of time, i.e. Sales from the Lunch period become Lunch Revenue. In Accounting terms, Cost is usually referred to as Expenses.

Cost Classification
In summary, Cost is Money or equal Value laid-out for **consumed** or **depleted** Goods or Services rendered; while Money or Value laid-out for **consumable** Goods is an Asset increase. (Inventory)

The term Variable Cost implies that Cost increases and/or decreases with Sales – while the term Fixed Cost is used for Cost occurring independent of Sales.

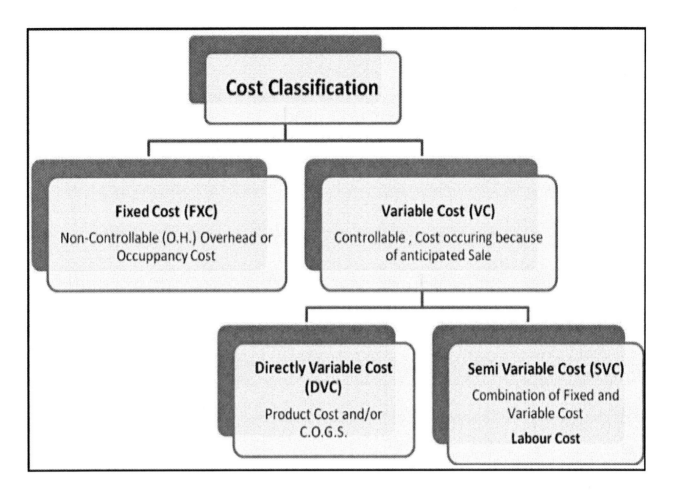

The term **Controllable** implies that it can be controlled within a short period of time. Example: If an unexpected increase in product cost occurs, it may be quickly offset by decreasing portion size or weight or product substitutions.

The term **Non-Controllable** implies that it cannot be changed within a short period of time. Example: A Lease or Mortgage can usually only be re-negotiated at the end of their term and not at will.

Most books I have read use the acronym FC for Fixed Cost. Throughout this publication I will use the acronym **FXC for Fixed Cost and FC for Food Cost** to avoid potential confusion and mistakes.

Blank space for notes:

The Basic Income Statement Structure
as of: dd/mm/yyyy

Net Sales, Revenue (without taxes)

minus C.O.G.S. Directly Variable Cost **(DVC)**

equals Gross Profit or Contribution Margin **(CM)**

minus Sales related Expenses or Variable Costs **(VC)**

minus Overhead Expenses or Fixed Costs **(FXC)**

minus Labour or Semi-Variable Cost **(SVC)**

equals Net Income/Loss or Profit or Loss or Alternative Cost **(ALTC)**

	A	B	C	D	E	F
1	**Basic Income Statement**					
2						
3	The Financial Statement for the "XYZ" Inn reveals the following information					
4	and figures for the year ending dd/mm/yyyy					
5						
6		SALES	Food Sales		0.00	Revenue
7			Beverage Sales		0.00	Revenue
8			Room Sales		0.00	Revenue
9		minus COGS	Cost of Food Sold		0.00	DVC
10	= GROSS PROFIT		Contribution Margin		0.00	GP or CM
11		minus	Cost of Beverage Sold		0.00	DVC
12		minus	Controllable Expenses		0.00	VC
13		minus	Overhead		0.00	FXC
14		minus	Payroll		0.00	SVC or FXC
15		minus	Payroll deductions~benefits		0.00	SVC or FXC
16		minus	Depreciation		0.00	FXC
17		equals	**PROFIT (Net income before taxes)**		0.00	ALTC

Now let's have a look at the same terminology for the structure of a basic Income Statement, with Revenue being converted to the shape of a Dollar Coin (Circle) and where all Cost are a part (Slice) of that Coin (Circle) to add up the Value of the Sale ($) or to 100%. **Think dimensional: Look at Sales as a Circle or Coin, representing 100%**

Any Costs allocated against Sales becomes a fraction of Sales – or if you like, a slice of a Coin.

Profit becomes a Budgeted Cost or Alternative Cost

Knowing that any or all Costs are fractions of Sales, the value of a fraction is easily calculated if the size of the fraction is know.

Management determines the size of the fractions based on the Business Plan and subsequent Budget.

The following are examples only. There are no standards implied. Each establishment based on the type of business they are, will set their own standard which is not comparable from one establishment to another. Within a chain of establishments one is tempted to compare, however cost of product and cost of labour as well as fixed costs will most likely be different based on location.

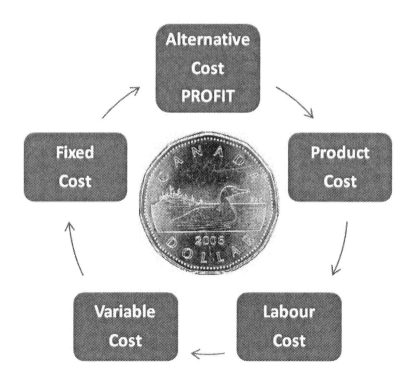

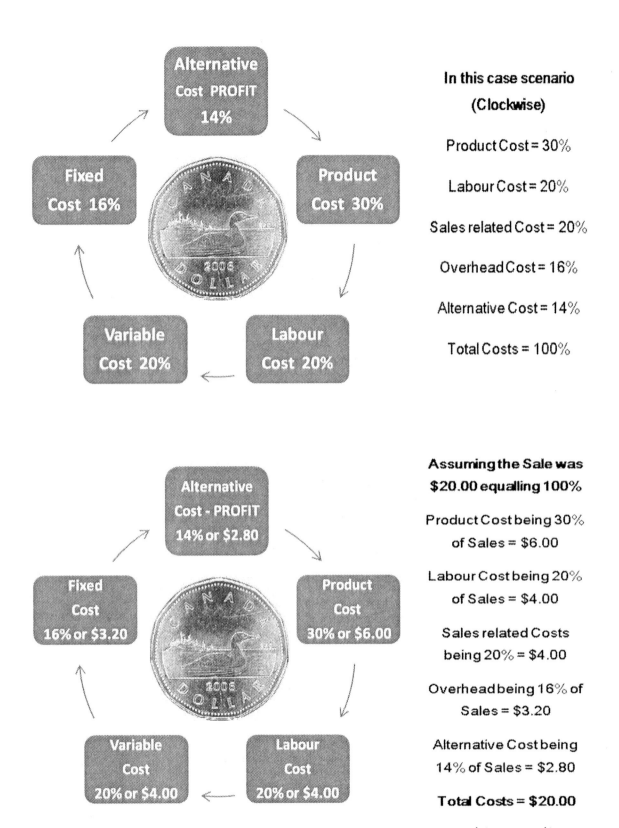

In this case scenario (Clockwise)

Product Cost = 30%

Labour Cost = 20%

Sales related Cost = 20%

Overhead Cost = 16%

Alternative Cost = 14%

Total Costs = 100%

Assuming the Sale was $20.00 equalling 100%

Product Cost being 30% of Sales = $6.00

Labour Cost being 20% of Sales = $4.00

Sales related Costs being 20% = $4.00

Overhead being 16% of Sales = $3.20

Alternative Cost being 14% of Sales = $2.80

Total Costs = $20.00

Formula used in this calculation: Sales x Cost % equals Cost in $ (S x C% =$)

Once all identified Cost have a percentage allocation assigned they become Projected Costs which must be closely and frequently monitored and compared to Actual Costs – if there is a difference between the forecast and the actual, it is referred to as a Variance which could be either positive, or negative.

Any **increase** in the Projected Cost(s) percentages or dollars however caused will result in a **reduction** of the Alternative Cost % and subsequently Profit.

Any **decease** in the Projected Cost(s) percentages or dollars however caused will result in an **increase** of the Alternative Cost % and subsequently Profit.

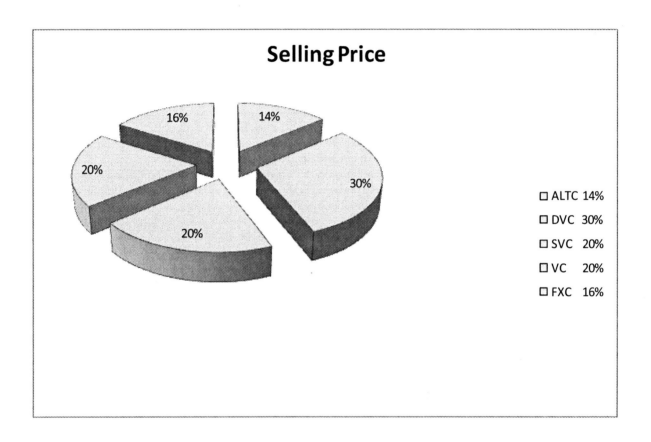

	A	B	C	D	E	F
1	**Selling Price**					
2						
3	Cost of Goods Sold			30%	6.00	DVC
4	Controllable Expenses			20%	4.00	VC
5	Overhead			16%	3.20	FXC
6	Payroll			20%	4.00	SVC or FXC
7	**PROFIT (Net income before taxes)**			14%	2.80	ALTC
8			Summary:	100%	20.00	Selling Price

Simplified Restaurant Revenue and Cost Areas

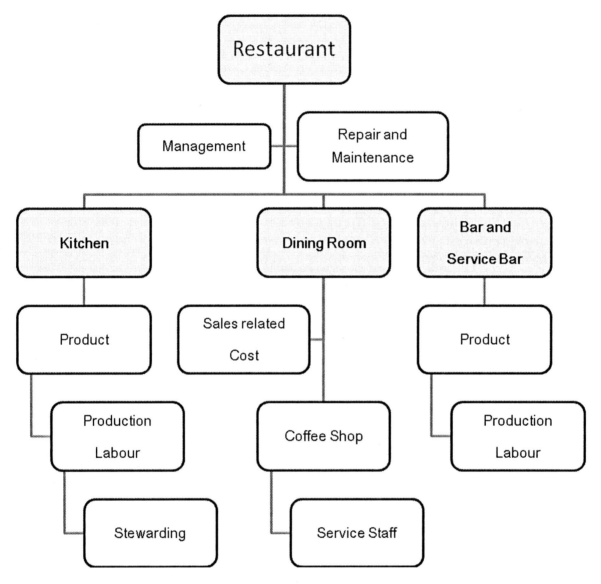

Looking at the simplified Restaurant, Hotel, Revenue and Cost Area Diagrams, the following should be observed:
Sales and Cost are calculated either as a Budget or Income statement for the whole Operation and for the Departments and their Sub-departments separately.

Example: Most Restaurants will have a Dining Room and perhaps a Service Bar, and/or a Sit-down Bar/Lounge. These areas are being served by the Kitchen.
Food and Bar Sales are usually accounted separately from one another.
Alcoholic Beverage Cost is allocated to the Bar. Bar Labour Cost may be allocated to the Bar or to the Lounge.

The Kitchen is accountable for Food Cost, Labour Cost, Stewarding and Equipment maintenance.

Management Labour Cost (Fixed Cost) and the Dining Room Service Staff Labour Cost (Variable Cost) are often allocated against Sales from Food and Beverage. There are no hard and fast rules and it is usually decided by Management.

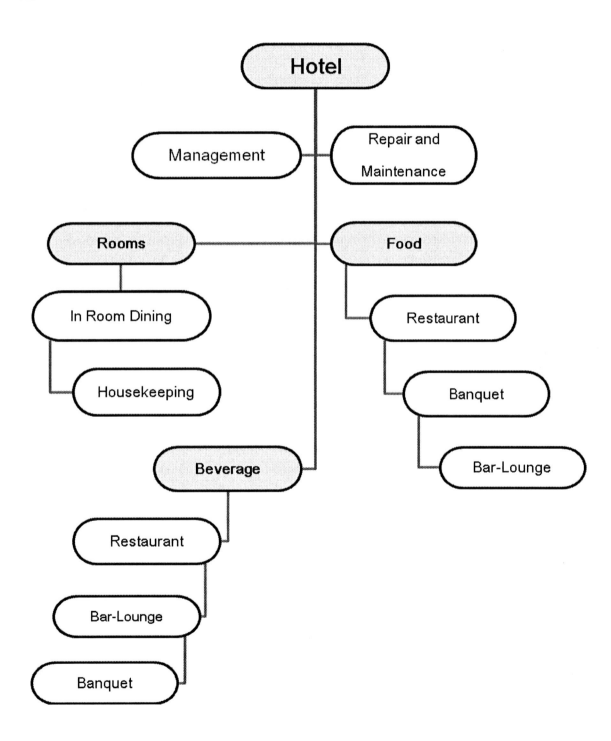

Simplified Hotel Revenue and Cost Areas

For Cost Control purposes, all Costs are calculated as a fraction of Sales (Revenue), the result being the ACTUAL COSTS, whereas for Budgeting purposes, Costs are established and subsequently SELLING PRICES are calculated based on DESIRED Cost percentage (%).

The two most common methods of calculating a Selling Price are GROSS PROFIT or PRIME COST pricing and DESIRED or IDEAL COST PERCENTAGE (%) pricing.

Lets calculate how DESIRED or IDEAL COST PERCENTAGE (%) pricing works:

PRIME COST pricing

Product Cost $1.50	Product $1.50 Labour Cost $00.75
Desired Cost 30%	Prime Cost 45%
P Cost 1.50	P + L Cost 2.25
div. by DC of 30%	div. by PC% 45%
= S.P. 5.00	= S.P. 5.00

In the above example there is no difference in the Calculated Selling Price – increase or decrease the Labour and Product Cost and recalculate. Keep track of the Results for comparison purposes.

Prime Cost may be calculated by department or for the whole operation, although most commonly prime cost is the allocated "Direct labour cost" to produce an item or items.

Example of Cost allocation: Sales or Revenue, are always 100% and Cost(s) are a fraction of Sales.

Food Sales and Prime Cost %

	Revenue and Cost from Food Sales	100%
1	Food Cost	28%
2	Labour Cost	20%
3	Variable Cost	20%
4	OH~Fixed Cost	20%
5	Profit~Alternative Cost	12%
	Total	100%

Prime Cost
= ~~FC %~~ + LB %
28% + 20% = 48%

Beverage Sales and Prime Cost %

	Revenue and Cost from Beverage Sales	100%
1	Beverage Cost	22%
2	Labour Cost	22%
3	Variable Cost	20%
4	OH~Fixed Cost	20%
5	Profit~Alternative Cost	16%
	Total	100%

Prime Cost
= BC % + LB %
22% + 22% = 44%

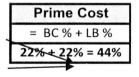

Example prepared by Klaus Theyer C.C.C.

Food and Beverage Sales and Prime Cost %

	Revenue and Cost from Combined Sales	100%
1	Food & Beverage Cost	25%
2	Combined Labour Cost	21%
3	Variable Cost	20%
4	OH~Fixed Cost	20%
5	Profit~Alternative Cost	14%
	Total	100%

Rows 1 and 2 → **Prime Cost** = 25% + 21% = 46%

Example prepared by Klaus Theyer C.C.C.

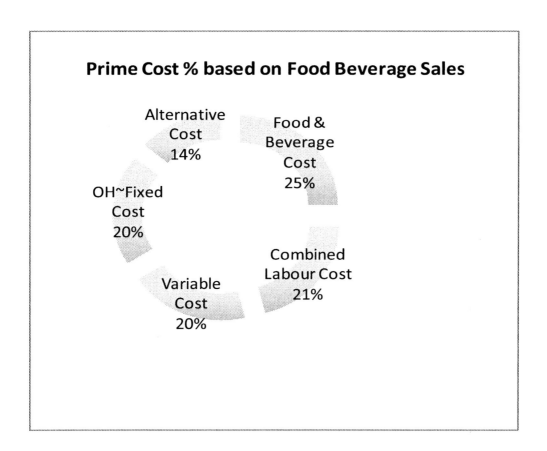

Prime Cost % based on Food Beverage Sales

- Food & Beverage Cost 25%
- Combined Labour Cost 21%
- Variable Cost 20%
- OH~Fixed Cost 20%
- Alternative Cost 14%

Example 1: To prepare a chicken stock, the ingredients cost $10.00 and the labour cost for the half hour it takes to set-up, skim and strain the stock is $7.50, the prime cost is $17.50.

Example 2: The food production area has a 30% Food cost and a 20% Labour cost then the prime cost would be 50%. If the Bar has a 22% Beverage cost and a 23% Labour cost then the prime cost would be 45%. For each example prime cost is calculated on their separate sales (100%).

If you were to combine the sales from the two (or more) different departments then the various product and labour costs would also have to be combined and the prime cost percentage (%) re-calculated.

Since Cost is a part of the Selling Price and directly influences Profit or Loss, it is expected that everyone working in the hospitality field is knowledgeable of what Cost is, how it occurs planned and otherwise, and how to check on/for it.

In order to communicate effectively, terminology was developed over the years to identify the different Cost applications. Some terms are more commonly used in the USA than in Canada and some terms are more popular in Canada. Since employees in our industry are often working abroad, it is beneficial to know as many terms as possible.

Think of Cost in relation to Sales and expected Profit. See for yourself how a small increase in Product Cost can affect Profit expectation

Selling Price of item:	= 100%	$10.00	= 100%	$10.00	= 100%	$10.00
- COGS	- 25%	2.50	- 27.5%	2.75	- 30%	3.00
= Gross Profit	= 75%	7.50	= 72.5%	7.25	= 70%	7.00
- Variable Cost (to Sales)	- 12%	1.20		1.20		1.20
-Semi Variable Cost	- 28%	2.80		2.80		2.80
- Fixed Cost	- 15%	1.50		1.50		1.50
= Profit (Net income (Loss))	= 20%	2.00	= 17.5%	1.75	= 15%	1.50

Management must monitor Product Cost, however since some menu items will have a higher Labour Cost than Product Cost and some Products will have a much higher Product Cost than Labour Cost, it is important to calculate the Prime Cost for each item sold. The Prime Cost is the combination of Product and Labour Cost.

Selling Price of item:	= 100%	$10.00	= 100%	$10.00	= 100%	$10.00
- COGS	- 25%	2.50	- 15%	1.50	- 45%	4.50
- Semi Variable Cost	- 28%	2.80	- 40%	4.00	- 15%	1.50
Prime Cost	= 53%	5.30	= 55%	5.50	= 60%	6.00
= Gross Profit	= 47%	4.70	= 45%	4.50	= 40%	4.00
- Variable Cost (to Sales)	- 12%	1.20		1.20		1.20
-Semi Variable Cost	- 28%	2.80		2.80		2.80
- Fixed Cost	- 15%	1.50		1.50		1.50
= Profit (Net income (Loss))	= 20%	2.00	= 18%	1.80	= 13%	1.30

A Chef's Companion to Cost Control

More Costs to be considered...

- ✓ **Direct Cost:** Cost of Product used and Service rendered.

- ✓ **Variable Cost or Sales related Cost:** Amenities, Condiments, etc.…

- ✓ **Indirect Costs:** Cleaning material, Linen and Uniform rental, Equipment maintenance, etc. These types of Costs are Variable Costs as they relate to Sales and are often referred to as Operating Costs.

- ✓ **Overhead Cost:** Fixed Cost, such as Rent, Mortgage, Utilities and Insurance, Décor (Flowers or Candles on Table), and in most cases Labour Cost including Benefits.

- ✓ **Semi-Variable Cost:** Total Labour Cost (Fixed & Variable, Full time & Part time employees) including Benefits.

- ✓ **Alternative Cost:** Expected Profit in Cost Calculations and Budgeting.

- ✓ **Capital Cost:** (Capital investment, any item, not for re-sale costing more than $100.00) Cost occurring for buildings, building material, chattels and equipment. Canada's Revenue Agencies view any Building addition, Chattel or Equipment Cost over $100.00 as Capital Coast, and therefore can only be partially (by means of depreciation) written off against Income.

- ✓ **Daily Food Cost:** Is calculated by dividing actual Cost of product used to make the Sales (Opening Inventory + Purchases – Closing Inventory) divided by Sales (Revenue) times 100 = Daily Food Cost percent %.

- ✓ **Historical Cost:** Cost occurred in a comparable time-frame. i.e. Last year's Mothers day Sales/Cost. This information is very useful for planning purposes.

- ✓ **Planned Cost:** Historical and/or other Cost information applied - Projected Cost.

- ✓ **Theoretical Cost:** Cost calculation based on Standard recipes (portions) not considering leftovers, wastage, over-production… Theoretical Cost must be compared to Actual Cost to establish the existence of a Variance which could be positive, or negative – in either case it must be closely monitored.

- ✓ **Ideal Cost:** Ideal Food or Beverage Cost is usually an Average Cost Percentage, based on Menu offerings which are achieving anticipated Profit.

- ✓ **Total Cost:** Accrued (accumulated) Cost within a specific time frame. i.e. Breakfast, Lunch or Dinner Service. Statement of Income and Expenses.

- ✓ **Advertising and Promotional Cost:** Cost occurring to Advertise and Promote your business to potential customers. Cost of Food and Beverage is allocated to the corresponding production areas and compensated for by crediting inventory with the value of the product used.

- ✓ **Staff Meal Cost:** This Cost is handled similar to the Advertising and Promotional Cost.

Anticipated, Projected, Desired, Planned, Budgeted, Forecasted, Target, Standard, Ideal, Actual & Variance, Documented, etc.

Throughout this publication you have been confronted with many Cost/Profit related terms which are not unique to the hospitality industry. In any industry specific expressions are being used to convey and discuss business matters in a professional manner. These expressions do change over time and new expressions are being coined frequently. What used to be Room Service is now often referred to as In Room Dining. The term Retained Earnings has been shortened to Retention by some users.
If attention is paid to what is said or written, terminology conversion is not that difficult to decipher.

Let's look at the term **Planned**. In order to plan something, a considerable thought process is usually followed;
Plans fulfill a **Desire**. **Anticipation** is used in the planning process. **Target**(s) is/are being identified. **Goals** are being set. **Standards** are being established based on perceived **Ideals**. This process is being **Documented**. A **Projection Forecast** is being prepared (in financial terms, a **Budget**). The **Budgeted Forecast** is compared with the **Actual** results, and any **Difference (Variance)**, positive or negative is being identified and analyzed for **Corrective** Actions (**Adjustments**) and for future planning.

Being COST conscientious!

"In order to be conscientious, one must understand and acknowledge"
One must constantly be on the look-out for COST. Recognize, monitor and control planned Cost, and look-out for Cost occurring which is not planned.

Sale - Revenue is always 100 %

COST is usually expressed as a **FRACTION** of Sale.
The FRACTION of Sale or Selling Price is commonly expressed as a Cost Percentage of Sale. The equation to calculate a **Derived Cost percentage** is: Product Cost or Cost of Sale, divided by Selling Price or Sale, times 100 equals Cost percentage.

Example: Food or Beverage Sale is $10.00.
Cost of Food or Beverage Sale is $4.00.
$ 4.00 ÷ $ 10.00 = .40 x 100 = 40.00 % (Food or Beverage Cost percentage)
C ÷ S (R) x 100 = C %

The same formula applies for Labour Cost percentage.
Selling Price calculation based on Cost percentage: **C ÷ C % = S.P.**
Cost calculation based on S.P. and C %: **S.P. x C % = Cost**
Cost % based on Cost and S.P.: **C ÷ S.P. x 100 = C %**

The before mentioned three formulas are the most often used formulas in Planning for Cost, Selling Prices and Cost control.

Selling price calculations using the Factor method:

The factor method is similar to the percentage method, however, instead of a percentage a fraction is used based on percentages. Assuming that what you wish to sell (Selling price equals 100%) or the number 100, the factor is calculated by dividing the percentage into 100. Example: The cost is $5.00, the desired percentage is 28%, 100 divided by 28 equals 3.571. To calculate a selling price using the factor method multiply Cost x Factor ($5.00 x 3.571 equals $17.855). In comparison, using the most common method Cost divided by Cost % ($5.00 divided by 28% equals $17.857). The difference between the two calculations is due to the rounding of decimal places.

	A	B	C	D	E	F	G	H	I	J
1	**Pricing Factors or Multiplier Table (expand to your own use):**									
2								by Klaus Theyer C.C.C.		
3	100%									
4	100	/	Cost %	Factor	Cost %	Factor	Cost %	Factor	Cost %	Factor
5	100	÷	15	6.667	21	4.762	27	3.704	33	3.030
6	100	÷	16	6.250	22	4.545	28	3.571	34	2.941
7	100	÷	17	5.882	23	4.348	29	3.448	35	2.857
8	100	÷	18	5.556	24	4.167	30	3.333	36	2.778
9	100	÷	19	5.263	25	4.000	31	3.226	37	2.703
10	100	÷	20	5.000	26	3.846	32	3.125	38	2.632

Other methods of calculating Selling Prices:

- **Based on Competition:** Not advisable to use, unless it is a very similar type of operation.
- **Based on Uniqueness of Product:** A very rare occurrence in our shrinking world of hospitality.
- **Based on Tradition:** No longer applicable.
- **Based on what the market will support:** If you can lower your menu prices in a bad economy, Customers may think you overcharged them when times were good.
- **Based on Loss Leader Principle:** Attract customers by offering menu items at a lower than usual price, hoping that they will consume more regular priced items.
- **Based Operators Profit expectation:** Self-explanatory. Sometimes not possible because of competition.

Cost behaviour as Business (Sales) Volume changes.

Demonstrated with two scenarios:

Scenario one; Employees scheduled for normal business based on reservations with unexpected guest arriving in large or fewer numbers than anticipated.

Staff Scheduled Numbers #	Staff Scheduled Value $	# of expected Customers	Ratio # Customer to Staff	Ratio $ per Customer	Change in # of Customers	Ratio # Customer to Staff	Ratio $ per Customer
12	$1,344.00	150	12.5	$8.96	180	15	$7.47
12	$1,344.00	150	12.5	$8.96	120	10	$11.20

Scenario two; Changes of Overhead cost per unit if more or less units than expected are being sold.

Average Overhead Cost per Month $	Average number of Units Sold per month #	Average Overhead Cost per Unit $	Change to: +/- Number of Units Sold #	Change to +/- Dollar per Unit	Difference +/- Positive Negative
$2,000.00	20,000	$00.10	25,000	$00.08	+ $00.02
$2,000.00	20,000	$00.10	17,000	$00.12 ($00.11765)	($00.02)

	A	B	C	D	E	F	G	H
1	Average Cheque		Month:			Day:		
2								
3			Outlet Name:					
4								
5		A	B	C	D	E	F	G
6		Number of operating days	Number of covers per day	Average food cheque($)	Average beverage cheque($)	Total food revenue (AxBxC)	Total bev. revenue (AxBxD)	Total cover per month (BxA)
7	List meal period							
8								
9	Breakfast	31	95	7.75	2.25			
10	Lunch	31	70	12.50	5.50			
11	Dinner	31	65	32.25	15.50			
12	Sunday Brunch	4	110	24.00	5.50			
13	Afternoon Tea	31	40	12.50	5.50			
14	TOTAL							
15								
16				Total F&B revenue:		(Total of E + Total of F)		
17				Total avg. cheque:		(Total rev. / Total # covers)		

C.O.G.S. Cost of Goods Sold:

When Menu Prices are being established the Cost of the Product is used to calculate the Selling Price. Depending on the Pricing method, sometimes Labour Cost is included to establish the Gross Profit (CM).

Although these methods are being commonly used, they will not provide sufficient information to evaluate and calculate Actual Cost and allow for comparison with Projected Costs and subsequently any Variance.

Business is required by law to take Inventory once a year but should at least take it once a month, although more often is even better for control purposes.

When a Perpetual or Physical Inventory is taken the Value of the Stock on hand is calculated based on purchase costs. This Value is recorded and used for the Actual Cost % calculation.

The equation is as follows:

Opening Inventory + Purchases − Closing Inventory = C.O.G.S.

C.O.G.S. ÷ by Revenue for this measured period calculates the Actual Cost %. The Actual Cost % is compared to the Projected or Ideal Cost % to calculate any Variances. (Positive or Negative)

The Projected Cost % is established by adding the Cost of each menu item and divide the total by the total from all menu Selling Prices.

Total Cost ÷ Total SP = Projected C %

C.O.G.S. ÷ Revenue = AC %

PC % - AC % = V % (Positive or Negative)

I.e. if the Projected C % = 29.00 %

and the Actual is   - 28.50 %

then the Variance is   + 0.50 % (Positive = subsequently good)

if the Projected C % = 29.00 %

and the Actual is   - 29.50 %

then the Variance is - 0.50 % (Negative = subsequently NOT good)

Although such a small Variance is not necessarily alarming, however, if the Budget is based on a Million Dollar Cost then the Variance is not that small anymore. ($ 5000.00)

Extended C.O.G.S. Calculation
Periodic Product Cost % Calculation

Transcribed by Klaus Theyer C.C.C. - inspired by David Jones C.C.C.

Period from: _____ To: _____   Recorders Name: _____

Production/Inventory Area: _____   Product Inventory: _____

	Food Production Area:		Beverage Production Area:	
	Opening Inventory ($):	1,500	Opening Inventory ($):	4,750
plus +	Purchase for Period ($):	2,750	Purchase for Period ($):	2,750
Equals =	Total available for Sale ($):		Total available for Sale ($):	
minus -	Closing Inventory ($):	700	Closing Inventory ($):	2,000
Equals =	Gross Product C.O.G.S. ($):		Gross Product C.O.G.S. ($):	
plus +	Transfers in Cooking Spirits ($):	250	Transfers in Food products ($):	150
plus +	Transfers in from other units ($):	50	Transfers in from other units ($):	50
minus -	Transfers out to Bar ($):	150	Transfers out to Kitchen ($):	250
minus -	Transfers out to other units ($):	50	Transfers out to other units ($):	50
minus -	Transfers/Promotions out ($):	100	Transfers/Promotions out ($):	200
Equals =	Cost of Product consumed ($):		Cost of Product consumed ($):	
minus -	Cost of Employees meals ($):	250	Cost of Employee beverages ($):	75
Equals =	Actual C.O.G.S. ($):		Actual C.O.G.S. ($):	

Actual Cost percentage calculation:

	Actual C.O.G.S. ($):		Actual C.O.G.S. ($):	
divided by	FOOD REVENUE	11,500	BEVERAGE REVENUE	25,000
Equals =	Product Cost percentage (%):		Product Cost percentage (%):	
	Contribution Margin ($):		Contribution Margin ($):	

Extended C.O.G.S. Calculation
Periodic Product Cost % Calculation

Transcribed by Klaus Theyer C.C.C. - inspired by David Jones C.C.C.

Period from: _____ To: _____ Recorders Name: _____

Production/Inventory Area: _____ Product Inventory: _____

	Food Production Area:		Beverage Production Area:	
	Opening Inventory ($):	1,500	Opening Inventory ($):	4,750
plus +	Purchase for Period ($):	2,750	Purchase for Period ($):	2,750
Equals =	Total available for Sale ($):	4,250	Total available for Sale ($):	7,500
minus -	Closing Inventory ($):	700	Closing Inventory ($):	2,000
Equals =	Gross Product C.O.G.S. ($):	3,550	Gross Product C.O.G.S. ($):	5,500
plus +	Transfers in Cooking Spirits ($):	250	Transfers in Food products ($):	150
plus +	Transfers in from other units ($):	50	Transfers in from other units ($):	50
minus -	Transfers out to Bar ($):	150	Transfers out to Kitchen ($):	250
minus -	Transfers out to other units ($):	50	Transfers out to other units ($):	50
minus -	Transfers/Promotions out ($):	100	Transfers/Promotions out ($):	200
Equals =	Cost of Product consumed ($):	3,550	Cost of Product consumed ($):	5,200
minus -	Cost of Employees meals ($):	250	Cost of Employee beverages ($):	75
Equals =	Actual C.O.G.S. ($):	3,300	Actual C.O.G.S. ($):	5,125

Actual Cost percentage calculation:

	Actual C.O.G.S. ($):	3,300	Actual C.O.G.S. ($):	5,125
divided by	FOOD REVENUE	11,500	divided by BEVERAGE REVENUE	25,000
Equals =	Product Cost percentage (%):	28.70%	Product Cost percentage (%):	20.50%
	Contribution Margin ($):	8,200	Contribution Margin ($):	19,875

Gross Profit Pricing:

Gross Profit (Sales minus COGS) is an Income Statement calculation and expression which can also be applied to individual menu items (Selling Price minus Product cost). Costs which are remaining are; Alternative, Fixed and Semi Variable Costs.

To apply this method, you must establish the Average Gross Profit for each Menu Item (Gross Profit divided by Number of Customers served).

Once this figure has been established, it is used as a basis for calculations.

Example: Gross Profit is $150,000.00. Number of Customers served during this period were 30,000. The Gross Profit per customer is $5.00. Cost of Product is $1.25.

(Gross Profit of $150,000.00 divided by number of Customers 30,000 equals Average Gross Profit per Customer).

Once the Average Gross Profit has been established the pricing method is quite simple. The Selling Price is calculated by adding the Average Gross Profit and the Cost of Product ($5.00 plus $1.25 equals SP $6.25). This method is particularly useful to achieve an appropriate Selling Price if the calculated menu items have a vast difference in cost.

Gross Profit Pricing example/comparison.
by Klaus Theyer C.C.C.

Name of Item	Cost	Desired C%	Selling Price	Gross Profit	Selling Price
Beef Consomme	0.87	18%	4.83	5.00	5.87
Vegetable Soup	0.25	18%	1.39	5.00	5.25
Birds Nest Soup	1.75	18%	9.72	5.00	6.75
Spaghetti	1.75	30%	5.83	5.00	6.75
Pastrami Sandwich	1.25	30%	4.17	5.00	6.25
Beef Steak	4.00	30%	13.33	5.00	9.00
Lobster	8.00	30%	26.67	5.00	13.00

In the above example different Desired Cost percentages were applied for the different menu items (groups). It is quite common to apply different percentages for offered items (groups) such as; Appetizers, Soups and Salads, Main Courses and Desserts, and Beverages.

At this point I believe I have covered the most popular methods of Selling Price calculations, however, as more books are read about this topic, as more methods you will be confronted with. The following are names and short explanations of methods to be considered:

Variable Cost Pricing:

Grouped menu items using different Cost percentages to calculate Selling Prices.

Combined and Product Cost and Labour Cost Pricing:

Similar to Prime Cost Pricing, exact Product Cost and exact Labour Cost for the produced menu item is used for calculation.

All and/or Actual Cost Pricing:

This method requires accurate and up-to-date Actual Cost information for the whole operation (Product Cost, Labour Cost, Operating Cost and Alternative Cost (Profit)).

All Costs are added and divided by the number of items produced, resulting in Selling Price for this item.

Cost Plus Pricing:

Similar to Gross Profit Pricing. Management calculated the Average Cost for each patron and the Desired Profit for each patron. By adding the two numbers and the Product Cost the Selling Price has been established.

One Selling Price Method:

This method of applying a Fixed Selling Price for each item in a group of items is often applied to menu offerings, such as; Soups, Salads, Desserts, main course groups such as; Pasta, Fish, Veal, Beef and of course beverages such as; Domestic beers, Imported beers, Domestic wines, Imported wines etc. This method discourages the consumer from selecting menu items based on their budget and allows them to pick and choose from same priced items within a category.

Although I am aware of other pricing methods, the purpose of this publication is to introduce you the most commonly used ones (Authors opinion) and I trust I have achieved that.

Labour – Payroll - Staff cost

Labour cost is perhaps the most difficult to control cost in any commercial foodservice establishment. Difficult to predict, since no-one ever knows what is on the potential customers "dining preference" mind, yet having the appropriate amount of staff on hand is perhaps the most important task for management. If the Staff to Customer ratio is too low, it may result in speed and level of service below customers expectations and un-happy customers, if the ratio is too high it will lead to increased labour cost affecting budgeted payroll negatively and may affect tip and bonus dependant staff adversely. This goes hand in hand with pre-preparation for goods to be sold and is one of the most common factors in Over – Under production. Record keeping of customer count, customer preferences, daily sales and conditions of sales such as weather, day of the week, holiday or other special days such as Mother's Day will provide a good basis for estimation of production needs and staff scheduling.

What makes up labour/staff cost:

Minimum wage; Is set by the various Provincial governments. In Ontario the minimum wage rose on February 1st 2007 from $7.15 to $8.00 per hour and is expected to reach $10.00 per hour within the next few years. There are different levels of minimum wage based on status (student under 18), adults and/or liquor servers.

Direct labour cost; Pay and mandatory benefits based on required skill level (**CPP**, Canada Pension Plan, **EI**, Employment Insurance, **WSIB** Workers Safety Insurance Board, **Vacation Pay**, **EHT**, Employers Health Tax). These mandatory deductions are subject to possible adjustments ever January 1st and July 1st.

Indirect labour cost; Absenteeism, Staff turn-over and training, Under-performance to standards, workplace accidents, Occupational Health and Safety Act...

Additional benefits; Profit sharing, Pension plans, Health related insurances, Performance bonuses, Commissions, Share options, Staff meals, Company car...

Employers Payroll Cost Example (Payroll January to June 2007); Employee "X" earns **$10.00** per hour and works 44 hours a week: **Gross pay = $440.00**

CPP = 4.95%	21.78	
EI = 2.52%	11.09	
Vacation Pay = 4%	17.60	
EHT = .98%	4.31	(.98% if total payroll is $200,000 or less)
WSIB = 2.41%	10.60	(Average Foodservice/handling Rate)
Cost of mandatory benefits	**$65.38 or 14.90 % of Gross Pay**	
Total Employer Cost	$505.38	(plus cost for payroll administration)

Actual employee cost per hour is: **$11.49** without any of the above mentioned other possible benefits.

Note: June 2007, announcement from the Ontario WSIB; the average premium rate of $2.26 per $100.00 of insurable earnings for 2007 will not change for 2008.

As previously mentioned Labour Cost is most commonly calculated and budgeted against potential and actual sales. Like all other costs, it is calculated as a percentage fraction of sales, see example pages 8 to 11.

Labour Cost Control is a process used by management to direct, regulate, and restrain employees' action in order to obtain desired levels of performance at appropriate levels of cost.

Labour cost is identified as a Semi-Variable cost (partially fixed – management, and partially variable – hourly paid staff based on projected sales). Most establishments where the payroll does not change in dollar value from pay-period to pay-period consider payroll a Fixed cost.

Labour cost may be calculated against; total sales, department sales, produced quantity, item, unit (plate), cost per customer…

Labour cost is directly influenced by the sophistication of menu items, level and type of service provided. The cost of employees rises with required skills level.

Labour – Staff cost starts with the hiring process:

Job-description; which clearly identifies the skill level and experience needed based on established Quality and Quantity standards of expected performance and subsequently determines the compensation level.

Want-ad; based on job description requiring candidate to submit a resume.

Selection for interview; offered to the most suitable candidates

Hiring and training; training cost occurs since both the trainer and trainee are not working to full capacity. A specific time frame needs to be identified, upon completion of training the trainee is expected to be "up-to-speed" based on the established performance standards.

Performance standard evaluation; based on Quality and Quantity standards of expected performance.

The illustrated Payroll calculation template on the next page is based on current prescribed benefits assuming that the Employers health tax rate is 0.89% and the WSIB rate is 2.41%. The most common WSIB rate for Restaurants and Catering is 1.65% for 2007 whereas the rate for Hotels, Motels and Camping is 2.65%.

The calculated average cost per hour based on the Base-pay-per-hour is $13.24 whereas the average cost per hour based on the Total payroll cost including benefits is $15.20. A $1.96 difference. Not considering this difference could lead to incorrect budget calculations with Profit infringing consequences.

This illustrated template and many others, will be available on www.MenuForProfit.com, please contact the writer if you would like to have it modified for your specific needs.

CANPAY 2007
Canadian Payroll Calculations

	A	B	C	D	E	F	G	H	I	J	K	L	M
3					Base rate	(equal)	Employer					Employees max C.P.P. for 2007 is 1,989.90	
4			C.P.P. =>		4.95%		4.95%					Employees max E.I. for 2007 is 720.00	
5	E.H.T. over 400,000 is 1.950%		E.I. =>		1.80%	(times 1.4)	2.52%						
6						Mandatory Benefits				Cost of Weekly Benefits $	Employee Pay per Week including Benefits	Cost of Benefits of each Employee %	Each Employee v/s Total Payroll
7	Employees Name	Base-pay per hour	hours worked	Total pay	Vac.Pay 4.00%	C.P.P. 4.95%	E.I. 2.52%	E.H.T. 0.98%	W.S.I.B. 2.41%				
9	Benjamin	18.50	44	814.00	32.56	40.29	20.51	7.98	19.60	120.94	934.94	14.86%	12.08%
10	Natalie	17.50	43	752.50	30.10	37.25	18.96	7.37	18.12	111.80	864.30	14.86%	11.17%
11	Rassani	16.50	44	726.00	29.04	35.94	18.30	7.11	17.48	107.87	833.87	14.86%	10.78%
12	Denesha	15.50	42	651.00	26.04	32.22	16.41	6.38	15.67	96.72	747.72	14.86%	9.66%
13	Siddharth	14.50	44	638.00	25.52	31.58	16.08	6.25	15.36	94.79	732.79	14.86%	9.47%
14	Dwayne	13.50	43	580.50	23.22	28.73	14.63	5.69	13.98	86.25	666.75	14.86%	8.62%
15	Yi Jung	12.50	42	525.00	21.00	25.99	13.23	5.15	12.64	78.00	603.00	14.86%	7.79%
16	Prashanna	11.50	44	506.00	20.24	25.05	12.75	4.96	12.18	75.18	581.18	14.86%	7.51%
17	Archimedes	10.50	40	420.00	16.80	20.79	10.58	4.12	10.11	62.40	482.40	14.86%	6.23%
18	Jheanell	9.50	41	389.50	15.58	19.28	9.82	3.82	9.38	57.87	447.37	14.86%	5.78%
19	Camilla	9.15	42	384.30	15.37	19.02	9.68	3.77	9.25	57.10	441.40	14.86%	5.70%
20	Ludwig	8.75	40	350.00	14.00	17.33	8.82	3.43	8.43	52.00	402.00	14.86%	5.20%
21	TOTALS:	157.90	509	6736.80	269.47	333.47	169.77	66.02	162.19	1000.92	7737.72	x x x	100%
22	Average:	13.24											

24	1.	Total hours worked		509				
25	2.	VAC Pay	each employee	See Column	E	or $ =>		269.472
26	3.	C.P.P.	each employee	See Column	F	or $ =>		333.47
27	4.	E.I.	each employee	See Column	G	or $ =>		169.77
28	5.	E.H.T.	each employee	See Column	H	or $ =>		66.02
29	6.	W.S.I.B.	each employee	See Column	I	or $ =>		162.19
30	7.	Total of Total pay					6736.80	
31	8.	Total $ of Total benefits					1000.92	
32	9.	Tot pay including benefits					7737.72	
33	10.	Actual Cost % of benefits					14.86%	
34		Avg. Cost per employee hour:						
35	11.	including benefits			Actual		15.20	
36	12.	without benefits			Actual		13.24	

WSIB 2007	Group	Rate % $
	207	4.35
	210	3.44
	214	1.87
	216	1.54
	220	4.01
	222	1.59
	223	2.36
	226	1.56
	230	1.54
	604	2.33
	919 R	1.65
	921 H	2.65
	Total	28.89
	Average	2.41

A Chef's Companion to Cost Control

Some easy and effective ways of controlling labour cost:
- Job-descriptions
- Selection and hiring process
- On job training
- Skilled supervisor/manager
- Standard recipes with identified production time
- Production and cleaning schedules
- Supervised Sign in and Sign out sheets
- Careful scheduling based on Sales forecasts and historical records
- Appropriate production equipment and facility layout
- Time-Punch clocks – Electronic Finger or Hand readers (Biometrics)

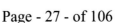

Payroll has become one the largest expense/cost in most food-service establishments. This adds considerable pressure to the Chef's responsibility of scheduling and maintaining a highly efficient workforce, often leaving insufficient time to train new staff and/or provide upgrading to existing staff.

A word about labour:
A topic where very little is written in text books dealing with cost, yet it is an instrumental part of cost control. Dishonest staff and Customers. This is a great concern of every employer. Many articles have been written about this topic and many seminars have been held trying to identify what makes a **cheat** and a **thief** and how one can protect themselves.

There are many things which can be done to deter a thief:
Screen potential employees during the hiring process. Provide clear directions (a written company policy dealing with theft) during the hiring process. Explain what is acceptable and unacceptable, how management practises prevention, and how unacceptable behaviour will be dealt with. Enforce methods such as approved purchase orders, frequent inventories, receiving records, limited access, cash control, locks and keys.

There are things which can be done to deter a cheat, which indirectly is a thief as well. Get informed about the various methods that can be used to steal. Understand all aspects of your point of sales system and read it frequently. Try to visualise how each employee is directly or indirectly exposed to the opportunity to steal – remove opportunities as much as you can without infringing on productivity.

The following part statistic is from the Rick Green eSeminars on Loss prevention website at www.ebridge.tv/LPG Mr. Green, General Manager of Loss Prevention Group, has been in the Security/Loss Prevention field since 1977 is an acknowledged and respected specialist in this field: The perfect situation for theft requires all of the following conditions: Opportunity, Need and Attitude. The approximate percentage of the population which will or have stolen if the conditions were right: "70%"
The percentage of the population who will always steal if given the opportunity: "25%".
Definitely something to seriously think about.

Calculation of Menu Item Cost:

Moving away from the managements point of view (considering all "Profit Centres") focusing on the operational aspects, let's look at the production areas (Kitchen/Bar). Controlling COST starts by identifying and calculating the COST of items offered on the menu.

A great deal of research based on Demographics, Competition, Popularity, Practicality and Profitability has gone into the selection of specific menu items, hence it is imperative to know the accurate cost of each item offered for sale to establish a Selling Price within the target Profit expectation. The chart below identifies Cost occurring and these cost are now being transferred on to a "Standard Recipe"

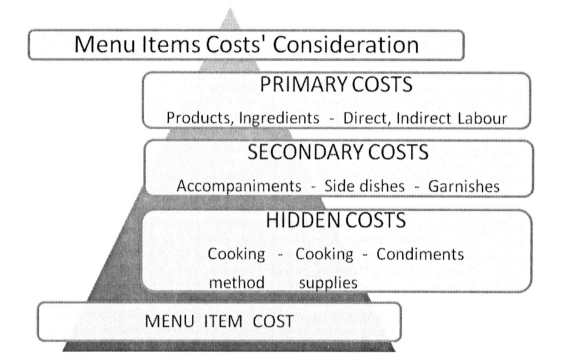

The Standard Recipe:

Standard Recipes are essential to establish and subsequently to maintain consistency in quality standards, by product description, quantities used, method of preparation, equipment and small ware needed, presentation-plating standard, quantities produced, portion or quantity yield, production time allotted, and method of costing applied.

The usage of Standard recipes is one way of ensuring that when repeat customers place an order, that they will receive what they have been accustomed to, time after time.

The Standard Recipe I developed and refined with the input from my industry colleagues features three pages – One for **Production**, one for **Costing and** one for **Presentation**/Plate design.

The following information is "common" to page one and two of the three page recipe.
- ❖ Page number # of #'s (1 of 2)
- ❖ Name of Recipe (Food or Beverage)
- ❖ Date (especially important to ensure updated pricing of ingredients)
- ❖ Service location; i.e. Dining room, Cafeteria, Bar. Lounge
- ❖ Recipe Category, type and number; i.e. App., Main, Dessert, Drink 101, 102,
- ❖ Source of recipe (to verify information)
- ❖ Portion yield and description (number, size, volume, weight, length)
- ❖ Direct Production Labour allocated; (minutes and skills based cost)
- ❖ A.P. name and type - precise description of ingredients used As Purchased
- ❖ Quantity description of ingredients **R.U. Recipe Units, as used in # and definition**
- ❖ Method of preparation (optional)
- ❖ Utensils/Equipment needed (optional)
- ❖ Additional recipes used, i.e. Sauces, Dressings, Stocks (finished products from another recipe)

The following Cost-calculation information is in addition to the "common" information on page two of the three page recipe.

- ➢ A.P. information – packaging-size-weight-volume-count-pieces-content
- ➢ Conversion from A.P. to selected R.U. (As Purchased to Recipe Unit)
- ➢ A.P. cost information (from invoice or extended inventory)
- ➢ Yield percentage % (to calculate yield adjusted cost and/or weight)
- ➢ Discretionary Overproduction, Spice, Ice and Waste Allowance (**OSIW**) in a percentage (# %)
- ➢ Additional Recipe A.P., Cost and Yield % information
- ➢ Input desired Selling Price
- ➢ Input Desired Prime Cost percentage
- ➢ There are optional Selling Price – Cost percentage and Gross Profit calculation tables available.

Once all information has been entered and verified, the recipe will automatically calculate the following results, in sequence:

- Labour cost
- Sub-Total and **OSIW** allowance
- Total Cost of Recipe
- Portion - Unit cost
- Gross Profit based on Selling Price
- Portion Cost percentage %
- Total Recipe Cost including Labour Cost
- Portion - Unit cost including Labour Cost
- Portion – Unit Selling price based on desired Prime Cost (P.C.) percentage %
- Optional Selling price, Cost percentage and Profit margin calculations

Although, the recipe may look intimidating at first glance, it is easily completed by using a step by step approach, completing the yellow high-lighted input areas and by following the suggestion in the automatic "help-boxes".

All information **except A.P. Info, Conversions and Yield percentages** should be entered on the Production page. Making changes to any of the three pages must be done on the Production page except changes to **A.P. Info, Conversions and Yield percentages** which must be done on the **Costing page**.

Page three, the Presentation page allows room for plate drawings or picture insertions. Each page of the recipe can be printed independently from the other pages.

Notes about the recipe (all pages): At the prompts to input or type information, enter in formation (overtype) where the input is. Example; Recipe name| Enter recipe name, start typing – over-writing the word Enter. I f information needs to be changed or updated, you may edit the field by locating the cell-pointer (cursor) on that field and pressing the F2 key, text can now be easily edited without re-typing. Numerical values and percentages should be typed over.

PLEASE DO NOT CUT, COPY AND PAST FROM ONE CELL TO ANOTHER. THIS MAY CAUSE INCORRECT RESULTS IN THE COSTING PAGE. IT WOULD BE BETTER TO OVER/RETYPE.

Blank space for notes:

Standard Recipe PRODUCTION Form

NOTE: YELLOW HIGHLIGHTED AREAS ARE REQUIRED INPUT AREAS Page # of #'s: 1 of 1

Recipe Name:	Enter Name of Recipe			Recipe Category:	Optional		Recipe #:	0
Date:	0	Service location:	if applicable			Direct Labour Requirements:		
Recipe Source/Reference:		Identify Source of Recipe (i.e. On Cooking page 862)		Production time in minutes ##	22	Average Labour Hour Cost $		15.00
Portion Size/Weight/Volume described =>		16 x 55 ml or 16 x 2 oz		All Recipe Units used MUST be stated in METRIC		Auto calculated labour cost:		5.50
Yield Portions # ==>	16	Recipe Units Described				Utensils / Equipment		

Product/Ingredient specified: (detailed product description)	R.U. used in #	R.U. used weight/volu/size	Method of preparation
Eggs, large	6.00	pc	Start typing here - text will wrap
Butter, unslated	450.00	gr	
Shallots	40.00	gr	
Sherry Vinegar	50.00	ml	
Wine, white, Riesling	50.00	ml	
Tarragon, fresh or marinated	45.00	gr	
Chervil, fresh	45.00	gr	
Bay leaf	1.00	pc	
Thyme, fresh	1.00	sprig	
Lemon, whole for juice	6.00	pc	
Pepper corn white crushed	0.00	TT	
Salt	0.00	TT	
13	0.00	0	
14	0.00	0	
15	0.00	0	
16	0.00	0	
17	0.00	0	
18	0.00	0	
19	0.00	0	
20	0.00	0	
21	0.00	0	

Additional Recipe(s) used:	used in #	weight/volu/size	
1	0.00	0	
2	0.00	0	
3	0.00	0	

Preparation & Presentation standards	694.00	<==== Total weight of ingredients divided by yield portions ====>	43.38

Start typing here - text will wrap

Recipe updated by:	Enter Your Name (type-over)		Recipe form designed/updated 2007 by Klaus Theyer C.C.C.

Standard Recipe COSTING Form

Recipe Name:	Sauce Bearnaise		Page # of #'s:	1 of 1
Date:	0	Recipe Category:	Optional	
Service location:	if applicable		Recipe #:	0
Recipe Source/Reference:	Identify Source of Recipe (i.e. On Cooking page 862)			
Portion Size/Weight/Volume described =>	16 x 55 ml or 16 x 2 oz	Production time in minutes ##	Average Labour Hour Cost $	15.00
Yield Portions # ==>	16	All Recipe Units used MUST be stated in METRIC	Calculated labour cost:	5.50

NOTE: YELLOW HIGHLIGHTED AREAS ARE REQUIRED INPUT AREAS

Direct Labour Requirements: 22

#	Product/Ingredient specified: (detailed product description)	A.P. Package i.e. Pieces Bag, Case	A.P. Package content # of Units	A.P. Package content Weight or Volume Unit #	A.P. Described Converted to Recipe Units # Weight/Volu.	A.P. Cost $	Yield % (if needed) %	Yield adjusted Weight	Recipe Unit Cost $	Recipe Units used in #	Recipe Units in weight volume/size	Extended Recipe Cost $
11	Eggs, large	case	180 pc	180.00	pc	24.70	100%	180.00	0.137	6	pc	0.823
12	Butter, unsalted	case	20 lbs	9080.00	gr	57.80	93%	8444.40	0.007	450	gr	3.080
13	Shallots	case/bag	3 lbs	1362.00	gr	5.65	90%	1225.80	0.005	40	gr	0.184
14	Sherry Vinegar	bottle	.5 gal IMP	2270.00	ml	4.95	95%	2156.50	0.002	50	ml	0.115
15	Wine, white, Riesling	bottle	.25 gal IMP	1135.00	ml	8.95	95%	1078.25	0.008	50	ml	0.415
16	Tarragon, fresh or marinated	bunch	.5 lbs	227.00	gr	2.75	60%	136.20	0.020	45	gr	0.909
17	Chervil, fresh	bunch	.5 lbs	227.00	gr	2.50	64%	145.28	0.017	45	gr	0.774
18	Bay leaf	open	leaf	1.00	pc	0.00	100%	1.00	0.000	1	pc	0.000
19	Thyme, fresh	open	sprig	1.00	sprig	0.00	100%	1.00	0.000	1	sprig	0.000
20	Lemon, whole for juice	case	120 pc	120.00	pc	10.50	92%	110.40	0.095	6	pc	0.571
21	Pepper corn white crushed	0.00	0.00	0.00	TT	0.00	100%	0.00	0.000	0	TT	0.000
22	Salt	0.00	0.00	0.00	TT	0.00	100%	0.00	0.000	0	TT	0.000
23	13	0.00	0.00	0.00	0	0.00	100%	0.00	0.000	0	0	0.000
24	14	0.00	0.00	0.00	0	0.00	100%	0.00	0.000	0	0	0.000
25	15	0.00	0.00	0.00	0	0.00	100%	0.00	0.000	0	0	0.000
26	16	0.00	0.00	0.00	0	0.00	100%	0.00	0.000	0	0	0.000
27	17	0.00	0.00	0.00	0	0.00	100%	0.00	0.000	0	0	0.000
28	18	0.00	0.00	0.00	0	0.00	100%	0.00	0.000	0	0	0.000
29	19	0.00	0.00	0.00	0	0.00	100%	0.00	0.000	0	0	0.000
30	20	0.00	0.00	0.00	0	0.00	100%	0.00	0.000	0	0	0.000
31	21	0.00	0.00	0.00	0	0.00	100%	0.00	0.000	0	0	0.000

Recipe form designed/updated 2007 by Klaus Theyer C.C.C.

			Sub-Total:	6.871
	Over-production, Spice, Ice, Waste allowance in %. Input # of % =>		10%	0.687
Additional Recipe(s) used:				
1	0.00	0.00	0	0.000
2	0.00	0.00	0	0.000
3	0.00	0.00	0	0.000

	Total Recipe Cost:	7.56
	Div. by Yield Portions, Insert # from above:	16
		0.47

Additional Selling Price calculation scenarios:

S.P. calculated @ a Cost % of:		C % calculated @ a S.P. of:		
C %:	= S.P. $	= G.P. $	S.P. $:	= C %	= G.P. $
15.00%	3.15	2.68	2.50	18.90%	2.03
20.00%	2.36	1.89	3.50	13.50%	3.03
25.00%	1.89	1.42	4.50	10.50%	4.03
30.00%	1.57	1.10	5.50	8.59%	5.03
32.00%	1.48	1.00	6.50	7.27%	6.03

	Input desired S.P. Selling Price ==>	2.50
	G.P. Gross Profit:	2.03
	Portion Cost %:	18.90%
	Total Recipe Cost including Labour Cost	13.06
	Portion Cost inc. Labour Cost:	0.82
Recipe updated by:	Selling Price based on desired Prime Cost %, Insert percentage here ==>	40%	2.04

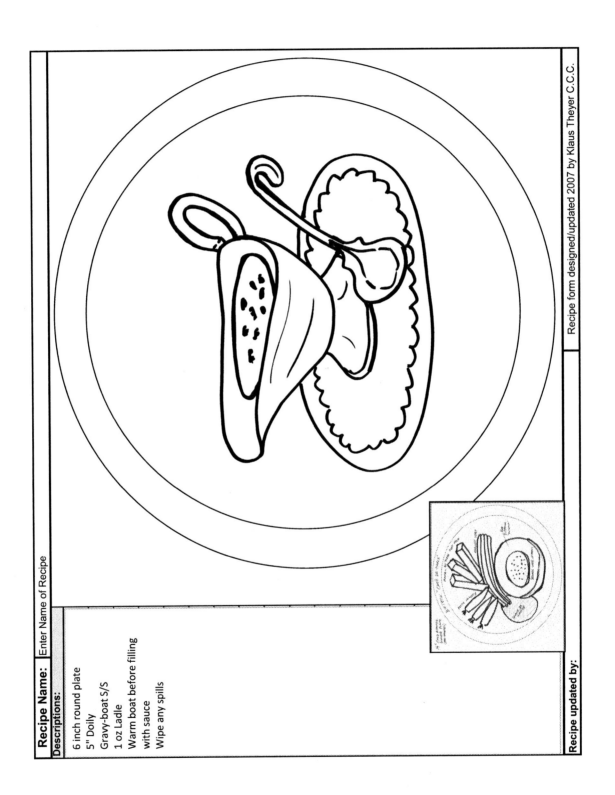

Recipe Name: Enter Name of Recipe

Descriptions:

6 inch round plate
5" Doily
Gravy-boat S/S
1 oz Ladle
Warm boat before filling with sauce
Wipe any spills

Recipe form designed/updated 2007 by Klaus Theyer C.C.C.

Recipe updated by:

The following One-Page Quick costing recipe is available for downloading from www.MenuForProfit.com. After inputting the Needed and As Purchased information the recipe will calculate the loss of product and increase in A.P. cost based on the yield percentage. The recipe also provides an area for Cost% and Selling Price calculations as well as Selling Price calculations based on Prime Cost.

#	A/B/C	D	E	F	G	H	I	J	K	L	M	N	O	P	Q
1	Recipe "QUICK COSTING" Form														
2	Recipe Name: Enter Name of Recipe														
3	Date: dd/mm/yyyy								Recipe Category:	Optional		Direct Labour Requirements:			
4	Recipe Source/Reference: Service location: i.e. On Cooking	if applicable							Recipe Number:	Optional		Production time in minutes			0
5	Portion Size/Weight/Volume described =>	Enter portion size/description here										Average Labour Hour Cost			0.00
6	Recipe Portions # =>	2										Calculated labour cost:			0.00
7		R.U. "AS USED"		R.U. "AS PURCHASED"			"A.P. CONVERTED TO R.U."		"YIELD CALCULATIONS"						Extended
8	Recipe Units R.U. "AS USED" described Product/Ingredient Specified:	Recipe Units used in #	Recipe Units in weight volume/size	A.P. Package i.e. Pieces Bag, Case	A.P. Package content # of Units	A.P. Cost $	A.P. Package content Weight or Volume Converted to Recipe Units #	Weight/Volu.	Yield % (if needed) %	Yield adjusted Weight Units	Yield adjusted Cost	Recipe Unit Cost $	Recipe Units used in #	Recipe Units in weight volume/size	Recipe Cost $
11	Butter unsalted	50	Gr	case	15 x 1 Lbs	45.00	6810.00	Gr	95%	6469.500	47.368	0.007	50	Gr	0.348
12	Eggs, extra large	12	pc	case	180 pc	16.45	180.00	pc	100%	180.000	16.450	0.091	12	pc	1.097
13	3						0		100%	0.000	0.000	0.000	0	0	0.000
14	4						0		100%	0.000	0.000	0.000	0	0	0.000
15	5						0		100%	0.000	0.000	0.000	0	0	0.000
16	6						0		100%	0.000	0.000	0.000	0	0	0.000
17	7						0		100%	0.000	0.000	0.000	0	0	0.000
18	8						0		100%	0.000	0.000	0.000	0	0	0.000
19	9						0		100%	0.000	0.000	0.000	0	0	0.000
20	10						0		100%	0.000	0.000	0.000	0	0	0.000
21	11						0		100%	0.000	0.000	0.000	0	0	0.000
22	12						0		100%	0.000	0.000	0.000	0	0	0.000
23	13						0		100%	0.000	0.000	0.000	0	0	0.000
24	14						0		100%	0.000	0.000	0.000	0	0	0.000
25	15						0		100%	0.000	0.000	0.000	0	0	0.000
26	16						0		100%	0.000	0.000	0.000	0	0	0.000
27	17						0		100%	0.000	0.000	0.000	0	0	0.000
28	18						0		100%	0.000	0.000	0.000	0	0	0.000
29	19						0		100%	0.000	0.000	0.000	0	0	0.000
30	20						0		100%	0.000	0.000	0.000	0	0	0.000
35	25													Sub-Total:	1.444
36									Over-production, Spice, Ice, Waste allowance in %. Input # of % =>					10%	0.144
37		Quick Costing Recipe Form designed/updated 2007 by Klaus Theyer CCC													
38	Additional Recipe(s) used:									0	0.000	0.000	0	0	0.000
39	1								100%	0.000	0.000	0.000	0	0	0.000
40	2								100%	0.000	0.000	0.000	0	0	0.000
41	3								100%	0.000	0.000	0.000	0	0	0.000
42	Additional Selling Price calculation scenarios:						S.P. @ Prime Cost % calculation scenarios:					Total Recipe Cost			1.589
43	S.P. calculated @ a Cost % of:	C % calculated @ a S.P. of:					S.P. calculated @ a Prime Cost % of:					Div. by Recipe Portions from above (C6)			2
44	C %:	= S.P. $	S.P. $:	= C %	= G.P. $		P.C. %:	= S.P. $	= G.P. $				Portion Cost		0.794
45	15.00%	5.30	2.50	31.78%	1.71		40.00%	1.99	1.19			Input desired S.P. Selling Price ==>			1.500
46	20.00%	3.97	3.50	22.70%	2.71		41.00%	1.94	1.14				G.P. Gross Profit		0.706
47	25.00%	3.18	4.50	17.65%	3.71		42.00%	1.89	1.10				Portion Cost %		52.96%
48	30.00%	2.65	5.50	14.44%	4.71		43.00%	1.85	1.05			Total Recipe Cost including Labour Cost			1.589
49	32.00%	2.48	6.50	12.22%	5.71		44.00%	1.81	1.01			Portion Cost inc. Labour Cost			0.794
50	Recipe updated by: Enter Your Name here						Selling Price based on desired Prime Cost %. Insert percentage here ==>							45%	1.765

A Chef's Companion to Cost Control

Definition of Unit and Unit Cost

A UNIT may be defined as the smallest dividable amount of the whole.

Example: A one litre bottle contains 1000 ml, hence the UNIT would be 1 millilitre. This may not be a very practical approach when it comes to gathering ingredients for a recipe, however, for cost calculation purposes it is the most accurate method of calculation..

Example: One (1) litre (L) bottle of Brandy costs $40.00, hence, one millilitre (ML) will cost $00.04. If you use 25 ML (5 US Tea Spoons) in the recipe then the **Extended Cost** (Unit Cost **x** Number of Units used) is $1.00.

In Cost Control, a UNIT may have a different meaning.
An assembled Plate of Food as promoted on the menu or a completed Drink is also one unit for the purpose of calculating how many items were sold or prepared for Sale. If you were to buy Eggs, 180 in a cartons (6 trays x 30 each) or in cartons containing 12 eggs, One Egg would be ONE UNIT.

If you were to buy Sugar in a forty Kilogram (KG) bag, then the Smallest Dividable Amount would be ONE GRAM. If however, you are in a large production situation, and recipes require a minimum of one KG, then of course the Smallest Dividable Amount for your operation would be one KG. For accuracy purposes, if practical, I suggest that you use the Smallest Dividable Amount in all your calculations.
Then there is the Unit of Labour Cost – it is important to allocate the appropriate Cost of Labour to calculate Costs – Example: Food production should use the Food Production Staff average Labour hour Cost including Cost of Benefits to calculate the total cost of food produced, which is then divided by the number of usable portions to establish the portion (Unit) cost.

Should you or your working environment still be stuck on Imperial or U.S. measurements, then of course the Metric examples based on the System International (SI) need to be converted. For your convenience you will find a Conversion table in the Tools and Workshops Section of this publication

Line/Plate Cost: A plate presented to a customer is usually an assembly of the main item (protein), side dishes (starch and vegetable) and perhaps a garnish (edible or inedible). The combined cost of these ingredients are referred to as Plate or Line Cost. For a simplified costing approach calculate the cost of each and all Side dishes and Garnishes. Divide this sum by the number of items used in this calculation, resulting in the Average Cost of one Side dish/Garnish. Calculate the portion protein cost, add the cost of the number of Side dishes/Garnishes used based on the Average Cost, and you just calculated the Line-Plate Cost for this item. **Easy enough? Yes. Accurate enough? Your decision!**

LINE COST by Klaus Theyer C.C.C.

Please calculate the LINE cost for using the following information!

	3	Side dishes

Conversion facts:

1 oz	28.375	grams
1 lbs	0.4536	kg
1 lbs	453.6	grams
1 Kg	2.2050	lbs
1 lbs	16	oz

Calculations must be extended/rounded to 3 decimal places

	AP info	convert to R.U. ==>		R.U.#	A.P. $	Yield %	Portion Size R.U.		Cost of additional ingredients used $	Total Cost
1	Carrots - Bag	25	kg	882.0	24.00	92%	3	oz	0.20	0.289
2	Spinach - Bag	0.5	kg	17.6	1.93	80%	3	oz	0.10	0.510
3	Cauliflower	10	lbs	4536.0	8.00	80%	80	gr	0.30	0.476
4	Green Beans	1	kg	35.3	4.50	92%	3	oz	0.20	0.616
5	Broccoli	1	kg	35.3	2.50	80%	3	oz	0.20	0.466
6	Brussel Sprouts	2	lbs	907.2	5.50	90%	80	gr	0.15	0.689
7	Potatoes	50	lbs	22680.0	25.00	90%	80	gr	0.20	0.298
8	Tomatoes Tray 24 pc	24	pc	XXXXXX	XXXXX	XXXXX	XXX	XXX	XXXXXXX	XXXXXXX
	One Tomato = 6 slices	6	slc	144.0	12.00	95%	3	slc	0.10	0.363
9	Rice Bag	10	lbs	4536.0	11.50	300%	35	gr	0.10	0.130
10	Pasta	1	lb	453.6	1.24	150%	35	gr	0.10	0.164

		Total => 4.000
		Avg. => 0.400

Total Cost of Portions?		4.00
Average Cost of Portions?		0.40
Line Cost average x	3	1.20
Main Item portion cost		9.04
Line cost		1.20
Total Cost		10.24
Cost percentage is:	32%	
Selling Price is:	32.00	

Yield calculations, their purpose and terminology explained

Yield is an expression used to identify the edible/consumable remains by adjusted weight and adjusted cost of As Purchased products.

A.P. (As Purchased)
Usually expressed as: Cost - Quantity (Weight - Volume - Pieces)
                            quality and Percentage %

A.P. is considered to be 100 % (the whole thing)

U.P. (**U**sable **P**ortion)
Refers to trimmed and un-cooked or to be cooked and not deboned product e.g. Ham, Leg of Lamb
Usually expressed as: Percentage % - Cost - Quantity (Weight - Volume - Pieces)
                              and in Quality.

E.P. or **Yield** (**E**dible **P**ortion - Consumable product)
Usually expressed as: Percentage % - Cost - Quantity (Weight – Volume - Pieces)
                              and in Quality.

The Edible Portion is the consumable remains of a product. The E.P. may be the same as the A.P., in which case the A.P. and the E.P. (Yield) is 100 %.
Conversely, if the A.P. product is being pumped, marinated, larded or barded, baked or steamed, or it is a Pasta or Rice product, then the E.P. (Edible Portion) may be larger or more in volume/weight than the A.P. product. In these situations it is advisable for Cost calculations to accept the A.P. Cost as the E.P. Cost, or as illustrated in the Line Cost example; calculation of the Yield adjusted cost or quantity.

Loss - The difference between A.P. and E.P.
Usually expressed as: Percentage % - Cost - Quantity (Weight - Volume - Pieces)
                              and in Quality.

A **Loss** of product may occur due to: pouring, mixing, spillage, spoilage and/or due to: trimming, cooking, condensing, boning, dehydration, slicing, carving, chilling, freezing, etc.
For mathematical purposes, it is most beneficial to know the **Yield** and the **Loss** expressed **as a percentage %.** Knowing the percentage will allow you to complete all necessary Yield and Cost and Yield and Weight calculations.

NOTE: Yield calculations **are not** necessary if **A.P.** weight and **Dollar** amount is apportioned into consumable units. e.g. A Strip loin weighs 4.5 Kg and costs $62.00 - trimmings (loss) equals .5 Kg, 20 steaks are cut from it, cost per steak is: $62.00 ÷ 20 steaks = $3.10 per steak (Unit cost).

Recipe Yield:
is the term used for the quantity or portions or units to be expected if the recipe is followed accurately.

Yield Calculations within a recipe example:
INFO: Purchased bag of Onions A.P. 40 lbs at a Cost of $ 30.00. The recipe calls for 10 KG peeled Onions. The Loss of peeling is usually 10%. How many lbs of Onions need to be peeled (with or without crying)?

Facts needed for calculation:
A.P. Weight (40 lbs)   A.P. Cost ($ 30.00)
Loss % (10%)   Yield % (?)

Conversion factor from lbs to KG (?) **Follow these Steps:**
FIRST: Covert A.P. Weight to Recipe Unit Weight (R.U.)
lbs x 0.4536 = KG   40.00 x 0.4536 = 18.144 KG (A.P.)

SECOND: Lets Calculate the Yield percentage by subtracting the Loss in KG from the Purchased KG and then divide the result by the A.P KG and multiply the result by 100 to achieve the Yield percentage:
18.144 – 1.814 = 16.3296 (E.P. KG) ÷ 18.144 =.090 x 100 = 90 % (Y %)

THIRD: Calculate the Usable Portion which is also the Yield by multiplying the A.P. KG by the Yield percentage.
18.144 x 90% = 16.3296.   I hope you noticed that you just made two different calculations , both yielding the same result. It would also have been sufficient to subtract the known Loss % from the A.P. which is always 100 % to obtain the Yield percentage (90.00 %).

FOURTH: Knowing the Yield percentage divide the U.P. weight (10.00 KG) by the Yield % to obtain the amount of Onions which have to be peeled.   10.00 KG (U.P.) ÷ 90.00 % (Y %) = 11.11 KG (A.P.)

In math there is often more than one method of calculation to achieve the same result. For accuracy I recommend to complete necessary calculations in more than one way.

In general and in the following example when calculating **Average (AVG)** Percentages – and **NOT only for Yield calculations** – the calculations should always be based upon **Totals,** i.e. The Total U.P. (Usable Portion) weight is divided by the Total A.P. (As Purchased) weight, times 100 to arrive at the **A**verage **U**sable **P**ortion Yield percentage of 86.667% (A.V.U.P.Y.%), Ditto for the E.P.Y.%. The Total E.P. KG is divided by the Total A.P. KG to calculate the Average Yield percentage (A.V.Y %). **Do not** calculate the AV Y% or the AV UP % by adding the percentages and dividing them by the number of units tested.

Cooking Yield Formulae and Scenarios by Klaus Theyer C.C.C.

File name: YieldPig

	A.P. As Purchased	U.P. Usable Portion #1	U.P. Usable Portion #2	E.P. Edible Portion
	represents 100% in Kg and $	Fraction of A.P. U.P. "1"	Fraction of A.P. U.P. "2"	Fraction of A.P. Yield
	As Purchased	Before Cooking	After Cooking	After portioning
A.P. weight	25 Kg	U.P. weight 24 Kg	U.P. weight 20 Kg	E.P. weight 15 Kg
		Shrinkage/Loss 1 Kg	Tot. Shrinkage 5 Kg	Tot. Shrinkage 10 Kg

A.P. Cost per Kg $5.50   E.P. Portion Size = 175 Gr

Total (extended) Cost A.P. = ($ per Kg x A.P. Kg) = $137.50

Loss between A.P. and "before cooking U.P. "1""
(A.P. weight - U.P. one weight) = 1 Kg   Loss % = (Loss "1" weight ÷ A.P. weight) 4%

Yield between A.P. and "before cooking U.P. "1"" =   (U.P. "1" Kg ÷ A.P. Kg) = U.P. Yield "1" 96%

Loss between A.P. and "after cooking U.P. "2""
(A.P. weight - U.P. two weight) = 5 Kg   Loss % = (Loss "2" weight ÷ A.P. weight) 20%

Yield between A.P. and "after cooking U.P. "2"" =   (U.P. "2" Kg ÷ A.P. Kg) = U.P. Yield "2" 80%

Loss between A.P. and "after carving E.P. Yield"
(A.P. weight - E.P. Yield weight) = 10 Kg   Loss % = (Total Loss weight ÷ A.P. weight) 40%

Yield between A.P. and "after carving E.P. Yield" =   (E.P. Kg ÷ A.P. Kg) = E.P. Yield 60%

As mentioned before, the purpose of calculating yield weight is to acknowledge the weight loss and to ensure compensation. **Example:** purchased 1 Kg of Pork leg at a cost of $5.50. Between preparation and cooking, the loss is 40% of its weight, or 400 Gr, therefore you only have 60%, or 600 Gr left for sale, but actually paid for 1 Kg (1000 Gr).

The formula for compensation is straight forward: (Divide A.P. $ with Y%) to calculate compensation for the Cost of the weight Loss.

A.P. $ p. Kg is: $5.50
Yield % is: 60%   Yield adj. Cost is: $9.17 per Kg

Based on the above example, we can now calculate the cost of one 175 Gr portion.
The Cost of one Yield adjusted Kg is $9.17 which equals 1000 Gr
Cost of one Gram is: ($ ÷ 1000) $0.0092 (9.17 ÷ 1000)
Cost of a 175 Gr portion is: $1.60 (9.17 ÷ 1000 x 175)

Another very useful application of Yield% is to calculate the Raw or A.P. weight to be purchased in order to serve a certain number of portions. **Example:**
You prepare for a function for 60 people, each one is to get a 200 Gr (E.P.) portion
You know from experience that the Average Yield % is 60% of A.P.
Equation: # of Customers x portion size, divided by Yield % equals weight in Gr.
((60 x 200) ÷ 60%) = 20000 Gr
divide Gr by 1000 equals Kg 20 Kg are needed to serve 60, 200 Gr portions.

Cooking Yield Formulae and Scenarios by Klaus Theyer C.C.C.

File name: YieldPig

	A.P. As Purchased	U.P. Usable Portion #1	U.P. Usable Portion #2	E.P. Edible Portion
	represents 100%	Fraction of A.P.	Fraction of A.P.	Fraction of A.P.
	in Kg and $	U.P. "1"	U.P. "2"	Yield
	As Purchased	Before Cooking	After Cooking	After portioning
A.P. weight	25 Kg	U.P. weight 24 Kg	U.P. weight 20 Kg	E.P. weight 15 Kg
		Shrinkage/Loss 1 Kg	Tot. Shrinkage 5 Kg	Tot. Shrinkage 10 Kg

A.P. Cost per Kg **$5.50**   E.P. Portion Size = **175 Gr**

Total (extended) Cost A.P. = ($ per Kg x A.P. Kg) = **$137.50**

Loss between A.P. and "before cooking U.P. "1"
(A.P. weight - U.P. one weight) = **1** Kg   Loss % = (Loss "1" weight ÷ A.P. weight)   **4%**

Yield between A.P. and "before cooking U.P. "1" =   (U.P. "1" Kg ÷ A.P. Kg) =   U.P. Yield "1"   **96%**

Loss between A.P. and "after cooking U.P. "2"
(A.P. weight - U.P. two weight) = **5** Kg   Loss % = (Loss "2" weight ÷ A.P. weight)   **20%**

Yield between A.P. and "after cooking U.P. "2" =   (U.P. "2" Kg ÷ A.P. Kg) =   U.P. Yield "2"   **80%**

Loss between A.P. and "after carving E.P. Yield"
(A.P. weight - E.P. Yield weight) = **10** Kg   Loss % = (Total Loss weight ÷ A.P. weight)   **40%**

Yield between A.P. and "after carving E.P. Yield" =   (E.P. Kg ÷ A.P. Kg) =   E.P. Yield   **60%**

As mentioned before, the purpose of calculating yield weight is to acknowledge the weight loss and to ensure compensation. **Example:** purchased 1 Kg of Pork leg at a cost of $5.50. Between preparation and cooking, the loss is 40% of its weight, or 400 Gr, therefore you only have 60%, or 600 Gr left for sale, but actually paid for 1 Kg (1000 Gr).

The formula for compensation is straight forward: (Divide A.P. $ with Y%) to calculate compensation for the Cost of the weight Loss.

A.P. $ p. Kg is: **$5.50**
Yield % is: **60%**   Yield adj. Cost is: **$9.17** per Kg

Based on the above example, we can now calculate the cost of one 175 Gr portion.
The Cost of one Yield adjusted Kg is **$9.17** which equals 1000 Gr
Cost of one Gram is: ($ ÷ 1000)   **$0.0092**   (9.17 ÷ 1000)
Cost of a 175 Gr portion is: **$1.60**   (9.17 ÷ 1000 x 175)

Another very useful application of Yield% is to calculate the Raw or A.P. weight to be purchased in order to serve a certain number of portions. **Example:**
You prepare for a function for **60** people, each one is to get a **200** Gr (E.P.) portion
You know from experience that the Average Yield % is **60%** of A.P.
Equation: # of Customers x portion size, divided by Yield % equals weight in Gr.
((60 x 200) ÷ 60%) = **20000** Gr
divide Gr by 1000 equals Kg   **20** Kg are needed to serve 60, 200 Gr portions.

Average Yield percentage (Butcher test):

Prior to selecting a supplier for meat(s) products, a Yield test should be conducted to establish the average shrinkage (Loss) and Yield based on supplied Quality:

A.P. KG Weight	Trim Loss KG	U.P. KG	U.P. Yield %	Cooking Loss KG	E.P. Yield KG	E.P. Yield %
10.00	1.50	8.50	85.00	2.00	6.50	65.00
9.50	1.20	8.30	87.37	2.00	6.30	66.32
9.75	1.20	8.55	87.69	1.80	6.75	69.23
Total: 29.25	Total: 3.90	Total: 25.35	Average: 86.667	Total: 5.80	Total: 19.55	Average: 66.838

To carry the previous example a step further by calculating the Yield ADJ (Adjusted) Dollar add the following information;
Purchase one was $ 12.50 per KG, Purchase two was $ 12.75 per KG, and Purchase three was $ 12.60 per KG. Calculate the Total Purchase Cost by multiplying 10 x 12.50 + 9.50 x 12.75 + 9.75 x 12.60 = $ 368.98. Divide this result by the Total A.P. weight and divide the result by the Y %.

$ 368.98 ÷ 29.25 KG = $ 12.61 ÷ 66.838% = $ 18.87. Of course, the same result would have been calculated by diving Total Cost A.P. by the E.P. KG.

$ 368.98 ÷ 19.55 KG = $ 18.87. Once again, in math there is often more than one method of calculation to achieve the same result. For accuracy it is recommend that necessary calculations are completed in more than one way.

Another method of calculating Yield adjusted Cost (Y.A.C.) is the **Yield Factor method**. Using the above example the Y.A.C. is $18.87 and the A.P.$ was 12.61.
Y.A.C. $18.87
A.P.$ $12.61 equals the factor (multiplier) 1.4964.

If there would be an increase in the A.P.$ (New Cost $12.75) multiply the New Cost with the Factor and voila, you have the new Y.A.C. or Edible Portion Cost.
$12.75 x 1.4964 = $ 19.08. This method saves you from re-doing the Butchers tests averages. This method will not be accurate if there is a change in the product or cooking method resulting in a higher or lower yield.

Illustrated below is a Butcher Yield test for Cooks.
An actual Butcher Yield test would focus on the usable/sellable muscle in proportion to Bones, Fat, Sinew, Collagen, reworkable and other trimmings to the total carcass.

	A	B	C	D	E	F	G	H	I	J	K	L	M
1	Butcher Yield Test by Klaus Theyer C.C.C.					Highlighted area are input fields.							
2													
3	Name of tester:							Date of test:					
4													
5	Name of Product tested:			Strip Loins Canada Prime									
6													
7				Grade:	Prime			Origin:	Canada (Alberta)				
8	NOTE: All calculation must be to no less than two decimal places!												
9													
10		A.P. Weight in Kg	A.P. Cost per Kg	Total Cost	Prep Trim Kg	Prep Weight	Prep Loss %	Yield % Prior	Cooking loss @ %	Cooking loss Kg	Yield weight	Yield %	Yield $ per Kg
11													
12	Supplier:												
13	1	7.2	$16.80		0.80				10.94%				
14	2	7.3	$16.80		0.90				12.50%				
15	3	7	$17.75		0.60				12.03%				
16	4	6.9	$17.90		0.40				10.00%				
17	Totals:								XXXXXX				
18												Average =	
19	Actual or Aver:												
20													
21	Average Cost of 1 Kg (E.P.):					Average Yield percentage % is							
22													
23	Best yield %				Supp. #			Best Yield Kg cost					
24	Based on the best Kg Cost,												
25	Cost of a	180		gramm E.P. portion is:									
26	The cost for all other ingredients (Side Dishes) is					1.95							
27				Portion - Plate Cost is				If the Selling Price is		$22.00			
28	Selling price based on a				27.00%	Cost is		The actual Cost percentage is:					

	A	B	C	D	E	F	G	H	I	J	K	L	M
1	Butcher Yield Test by Klaus Theyer C.C.C.					Highlighted area are input fields.							
2													
3	Name of tester:							Date of test:					
4													
5	Name of Product tested:			Strip Loins Canada Prime									
6													
7				Grade:	Prime			Origin:	Canada (Alberta)				
8	NOTE: All calculation must be to no less than two decimal places!												
9													
10		A.P. Weight in Kg	A.P. Cost per Kg	Total Cost	Prep Trim Kg	Prep Weight	Prep Loss %	Yield % Prior	Cooking loss @ %	Cooking loss Kg	Yield weight	Yield %	Yield $ per Kg
11													
12	Supplier:												
13	1	7.2	$16.80	$120.96	0.80	6.4	11.11%	88.89%	10.94%	0.70	5.70	79.17%	$21.22
14	2	7.3	$16.80	$122.64	0.90	6.4	12.33%	87.67%	12.50%	0.80	5.60	76.71%	$21.90
15	3	7	$17.75	$124.25	0.60	6.4	8.57%	91.43%	12.03%	0.77	5.63	80.43%	$22.07
16	4	6.9	$17.90	$123.51	0.40	6.5	5.80%	94.20%	10.00%	0.65	5.85	84.78%	$21.11
17	Totals:	28.40	$69.25	$491.36	2.70	25.70			XXXXXX	2.920	22.78		$86.30
18												Average =	$21.58
19	Actual or Aver:	7.100	17.31	122.84	0.675	6.425	9.51%	90.493%	11.36%	0.730	5.695	80.211%	
20													
21	Average Cost of 1 Kg (E.P.):			$86.303		Average Yield percentage % is			80.211%				
22													
23	Best yield %	84.78%			Supp. #	4		Best Yield Kg cost		$21.113			
24	Based on the best Kg Cost,												
25	Cost of a	180		gramm E.P. portion is:		3.80							
26	The cost for all other ingredients (Side Dishes) is					1.95							
27				Portion - Plate Cost is		5.75		If the Selling Price is		$22.00			
28	Selling price based on a				27.00%	Cost is	21.297	The actual Cost percentage is:		26.14%			

Intro to BUDGETS and Budgeting:

"A Budget should be a **Realistic** expression of **Goals and Objectives** in Financial Terms."

A budget, to be meaningful, must be based on realistic, achievable, goals and objectives, considering all related factors. A budget could be as simple as dealing with one item, i.e., Item: Staffing level base on Occupancy, or as complex as a business plan. Of course there are many factors to be considered before engaging a calculator.

First and most important, is the time/period. The shortest time period (to be practical) should not be less than one week, and the longest time period not longer than five years. However, it is not unheard of, to prepare budgets for one day, or for a longer time span than five years.

Usually, budgets are prepared for all departments within a business, and for different time periods. It is not uncommon to look ahead and determine where the business (financially) should be in five years from now. This is usually done with a **LONG TERM** budget. Of course, history has taught us that long term budgets may be rendered un-achievable due to recession or unforeseen circumstances, or on the contrary, they are too conservative in economic upward trends.

Therefore, every long term budget should be the guideline for **SHORT TERM** budgets. Businesses prepare annual budgets, based on their fiscal year, conforming to the long term goals and objectives. Once business has established its **LONG TERM** goals, this becomes the **MASTER** budget. Subsequent **SHORT TERM** budgets must remain **FLEXIBLE** to conform to the long term goals.

Common types of Budgets:
Long term, Short term, Capital (Balance sheet items; cash flow budget, capital equipment replacement (Asset)), Operating (ongoing projection of Revenue and Expenditures), Departmental (Forecasted Revenue and Expenditures based on one department, i.e., Food, Beverage), Master (most comprehensive, for one year or more, including balance sheet and income/expenses from all departments), Fixed (based on one level of activity or revenue - and estimated expenses are based on this level of revenue. i.e., Sales for the year are $XXX.XX dollars on the average, and Prime cost is based on an average percentage % - if Sales unexpectedly in-or-decrease, it is difficult to make immediate monetary adjustments to this situation).

> **Simple, but very important equations:**
> If COST (other then Alternative Cost) is more than Sales, a LOSS will occur.
> If COST (other then Alternative Cost) is less than Sales, a PROFIT is achieved.
> If Cost (not including Alternative Cost) equals Sales the "Break-Even-Point" has been reached.
> Every business needs to know at what level of Sales the "Break-Even-Point" will be reached.

Top-Down; from a Long-term Master Budget allocation to Department, covering a period of one year, apportioned to one month. Period adjustments are made to conform to the Long-Term-Goal.

Bottom-Up; From daily Departmental sales to Weekly-Monthly to Annual in order to build a Long-Term-Budget.

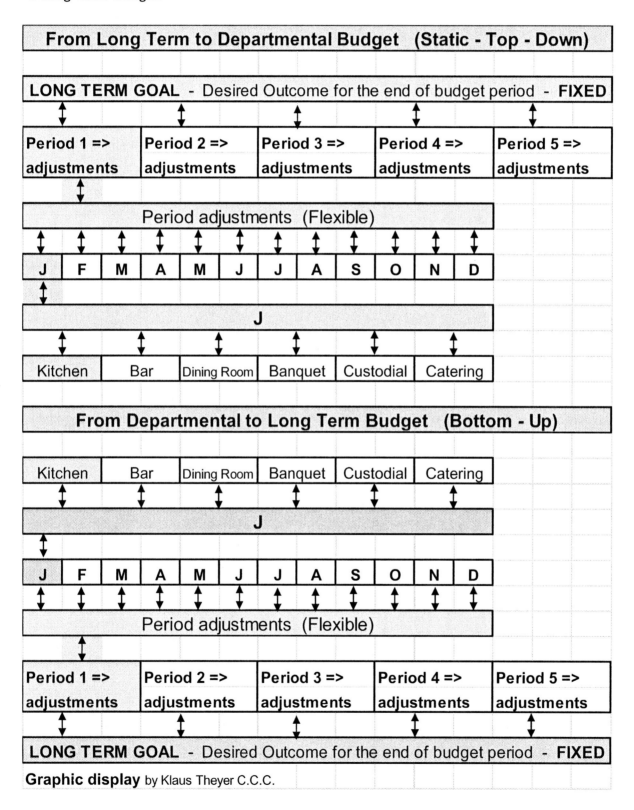

Graphic display by Klaus Theyer C.C.C.

Budgets are used:
To project achievable levels of Sales (the increase must at least cover projected inflation)
To establish **Standards or Targets** for Dollar expenditures...
To provide a Standard against which Expenditures can be measured...
To establish Limits for Expenditures, and thus to restrict the amounts that can be spent for particular purposes..
to compare **actual against planned**, analyze the difference, **(variances)** and take corrective actions.

Note:
Budgeting set not only **Goals and Objectives**, it may also be **Restrictive** and therefore may have **negative connotations**, particularly to middle-management employees. Effects can be frustrating and demoralizing.

"A Budget is a common Control technique."

Common types of Budgets:
STATIC - for one level of business activity (Fixed Sales - Fixed Costs)

FLEXIBLE - prepared for more than one level of business activity,
Adjusted to Sales - Costs.

ZBB - Zero based Budgeting - All budgeted administrative, marketing, property operation and maintenance, energy costs and general expenses - have to be justified by each department.

Types of Budgets for Specific Aspects of Operation:
Operation Budget - Sales Budget...
Cash Flow Budget - Capital Equipment - Replacement...
Repair and Maintenance - Advertising and Promotion...
Product and Labour...

Most important is the Operating Budget - it is a Forecast of Sales and an Estimation of Costs to earn Sales.
By extension, the Budget suggest the Profit that should result after the Costs of producing those Sales have been met.

Corporate budget:
For years, most companies have taken a inflexible, centralized approach to budget planning and forecasting. But businesses are making big changes in their budget planning and forecasting processes. Once carried out by a CFO (Chief Financial Officer) and accountants. Budget planning today has becom more of a companywide effort, with a greater number of managers and employees contributing to the process.
Many companies are striving to combine the traditional bottom-up approach to budget preparation, in which department heads submit budget requests that are combined into a corporate budget, with a top-down approach in which budgets are prepared in conjunction with planned objectives as outlined by management.

Annual budgets were once as unchanging as a statue, more companies now view budgets as living documents subject to revisions on an ongoing basis throughout the year.

	A	B	C	D	E	F	G	H	I	J
1										
2				Budget based on Income Statement					Variance Increase/Decrease from This to Next year	
3										
4					This year	%	Next year	%	(+/-) $	(+/-) %
5				Revenue						
6				Food Sales	1,533,564		1,728,020			
7				Catering Sales	357,447		330,356			
8				Total Food Sales						
9				Beverage Sales	415,099		482,830			
10				Total Sales~Revenue		100.00%		100.00%		
11										
12				Cost of Goods Sold						
13				Meat, Seafood	297,488		343,063			
14				Fruits, Vegetable	94,550		127,060			
15				Dairy	55,347		40,660			
16				Baked Goods	16,142		22,870			
17				Dry Goods	249,060		233,790			
18				Total Cost of Food sold						
19				Wine Domestic & Imported	42,400		48,760			
20				Beer Domestic & Imported	29,550		26,596			
21				Hard Liquor	22,600		21,210			
22				Total Cost of Beverage sold						
23				Total COGS						
24				Gross Profit						
25										
26				Operating Expenses (Costs)						
27				Salaries & Wages	641,099		710,585			
28				Mandatory Benefits	168,346		190,590			
29				Total Payroll & related						
30				Direct Operating (Occupancy) expenses	142,309		180,200			
31				Marketing	89,622		99,189			
32				Energy & Utility services	121,000		119,500			
33				Administrative & General	66,000		70,541			
34				Repairs and Maintenance	17,861		29,520			
35				Total Operating expenses						
36										
37				Income before Rent, Interest & Depreciation						
38				Fixed Expenses (Costs OH)						
39				Rent/Interest	86,750		84,889			
40				Depreciation	80,496		82,183			
41				Total Fixed expenses						
42										
43				Net Income (Loss)						

A Chef's Companion to Cost Control

Budget based on Income Statement

	This year	%	Next year	%	Variance Increase/Decrease from This to Next year	
					(+/-) $	(+/-) %
Revenue						
Food Sales	1,533,564	66.50%	1,728,020	68.00%	194,456	12.68%
Catering Sales	357,447	15.50%	330,356	13.00%	(27,091)	-7.58%
Total Food Sales	1,891,011	82.00%	2,058,376	81.00%	167,365	8.85%
Beverage Sales	415,099	18.00%	482,830	19.00%	67,731	16.32%
Total Sales~Revenue	**2,306,110**	**100.00%**	**2,541,206**	**100.00%**	**235,096**	**10.19%**
Cost of Goods Sold						
Meat, Seafood	297,488	15.73%	343,063	16.67%	45,575	15.32%
Fruits, Vegetable	94,550	5.00%	127,060	6.17%	32,510	34.38%
Dairy	55,347	2.93%	40,660	1.98%	(14,687)	-26.54%
Baked Goods	16,142	0.85%	22,870	1.11%	6,728	41.68%
Dry Goods	249,060	13.17%	233,790	11.36%	(15,270)	-6.13%
Total Cost of Food sold	712,587	37.68%	767,443	37.28%	54,856	7.70%
Wine Domestic & Imported	42,400	10.21%	48,760	10.10%	6,360	15.00%
Beer Domestic & Imported	29,550	7.12%	26,596	5.51%	(2,954)	-10.00%
Hard Liquor	22,600	5.44%	21,210	4.39%	(1,390)	-6.15%
Total Cost of Beverage sold	94,550	22.78%	96,566	20.00%	2,016	2.13%
Total COGS	807,137	35.00%	864,009	34.00%	56,872	7.05%
Gross Profit	**1,498,973**	**65.00%**	**1,677,197**	**66.00%**	**178,224**	**11.89%**
Operating Expenses (Costs)						
Salaries & Wages	641,099	27.80%	710,585	27.96%	69,486	10.84%
Mandatory Benefits	168,346	7.30%	190,590	7.50%	22,244	13.21%
Total Payroll & related	809,445	35.10%	901,175	35.46%	91,730	11.33%
Direct Operating (Occupancy) expenses	142,309	6.17%	180,200	7.09%	37,891	26.63%
Marketing	89,622	3.89%	99,189	3.90%	9,567	10.67%
Energy & Utility services	121,000	5.25%	119,500	4.70%	(1,500)	-1.24%
Administrative & General	66,000	2.86%	70,541	2.78%	4,541	6.88%
Repairs and Maintenance	17,861	0.77%	29,520	1.16%	11,659	65.28%
Total Operating expenses	1,246,237	54.04%	1,400,125	55.10%	153,888	12.35%
Income before Rent, Interest & Depreciation	**252,736**	**10.96%**	**277,072**	**10.90%**	**24,336**	**9.63%**
Fixed Expenses (Costs OH)						
Rent/Interest	86,750	3.76%	84,889	3.34%	(1,861)	-2.15%
Depreciation	80,496	3.49%	82,183	3.23%	1,687	2.10%
Total Fixed expenses	167,246	7.25%	167,072	6.57%	(174)	-0.10%
Net Income (Loss)	**85,490**	**3.71%**	**110,000**	**4.33%**	**24,510**	**28.67%**

The Operations Budget

Manager ~ Chef's responsibility fully or partially

Revenue (Sales):
Food Sales:
Beverage Sales:

COGS (DVC):
Cost of Food:
Cost of Beverage:

Labour Cost (SVC):
Food Production:
Dining-Bar:
Non-production labour:

Variable Cost (VC):

Fixed Costs (FXC):

Profit/Loss: (Alternative Cost)

Food Sales: Menu planning, writing, design....

Cost of Food: Recipe accuracy, Purchasing frequency & quantity, Production planning, Wastage, Theft, Staff meals, Spoilage, Over/Under production....

Labour: Hiring, Scheduling, Accident prevention, Leadership, Productivity....

VC: Uniforms, Knife sharpening, Condiments....

FXC: May have proportional share allocated....

Budget from the Old French bougette, diminutive of bouge, small leather bag, from Latin bulga, of Celtic origin meaning little bag to Middle English bouget, wallet, generally refers to a list of all planned expenses and revenues. A budget is an important concept in microeconomics, which uses a budget line to illustrate the trade-offs between two or more goods.

1. An itemized summary of estimated or intended expenditures for a given period along with proposals for financing them
2. An itemized summary of intended expenditure
3. The total sum of money allocated for a particular purpose or period of time

2006 Budget based on Income Statement with Break even Point calculation.

	Type of SALE or COST	This year	Next year	Variance Increase/Decrease from THIS to NEXT year	
				(+/-) $	(+/-) %
Revenue					
Food Sales	Rev/FS	1,533,564	1,700,000	166,436	10.85%
Catering Sales	Rev/FS	357,447	350,000		
Total Food Sales	Rev/FS				
Beverage Sales	Rev/BS	415,099	430,000		
	REV				
Cost of Goods Sold					
Meat, Seafood	VC/DVC	297,488	310,000		
Fruits, Vegetable	VC/DVC	94,550	110,000		
Dairy	VC/DVC	55,347	50,000		
Baked Goods	VC/DVC	16,142	20,000		
Dry Goods	VC/DVC	249,060	240,000		
Total Cost of Food Sold	VC/DVC				
Wine Domestic & Imported	VC/DVC	42,400	49,000		
Beer Domestic & Imported	VC/DVC	29,550	26,000		
Hard Liquor	VC/DVC	22,600	20,000		
Total Cost of Beverage Sold	VC/DVC				
Total COGS	**COGS**				
Gross Profit	**GP/CM**				
Operating Expenses (Costs)					
Wages (hourly)	VC/SVC	395,450	420,000		
Mandatory Benefits (hourly)	VC/SVC	71,182	75,600		
Hourly Payroll and Benefits	VC/SVC				
Direct Operating expenses	VC	142,309	150,000		
Marketing	VC	89,622	95,000		
Administrative & General	VC	66,000	70,000		
Total Operating expenses	**VC**				
Fixed Expenses, Overhead, Occupancy Cost					
Wages managerial	FXC	122,540	150,000		
Mandatory and other Benefits	FXC	26,959	33,000		
Energy & Utility services	FXC	121,000	125,000		
Rent/Interest	FXC	86,750	88,000		
Depreciation	FXC	80,496	83,000		
Total Fixed Expenses	**FXC**				
Profit, Net Income/Loss	**P/NI/L**				

Break Even Point Calculations

BEP for THIS year:		BEP for NEXT year:	
Sales:		Sales:	
Variable Costs:		Variable Costs:	
Fixed Costs:		Fixed Costs:	
VR= (VC/S):		VR= (VC/S):	
CR=(1-VR):		CR=(1-VR):	
BEP (FXC/CR)		**BEP (FXC/CR)**	

2006 Budget based on Income Statement with Break even Point calculation.

	Type of SALE or COST	This year	Next year	Variance Increase/Decrease from THIS to NEXT year	
				(+/-) $	(+/-) %
Revenue					
Food Sales	Rev/FS	1,533,564	1,700,000	166,436	10.85%
Catering Sales	Rev/FS	357,447	350,000	-7,447	-2.08%
Total Food Sales	Rev/FS	1,891,011	2,050,000	158,989	8.41%
Beverage Sales	Rev/BS	415,099	430,000	14,901	3.59%
	REV	2,306,110	2,480,000	173,890	7.54%
Cost of Goods Sold					
Meat, Seafood	VC/DVC	297,488	310,000	12,512	4.21%
Fruits, Vegetable	VC/DVC	94,550	110,000	15,450	16.34%
Dairy	VC/DVC	55,347	50,000	-5,347	-9.66%
Baked Goods	VC/DVC	16,142	20,000	3,858	23.90%
Dry Goods	VC/DVC	249,060	240,000	-9,060	-3.64%
Total Cost of Food Sold	VC/DVC	712,587	730,000	17,413	2.44%
Wine Domestic & Imported	VC/DVC	42,400	49,000	6,600	15.57%
Beer Domestic & Imported	VC/DVC	29,550	26,000	-3,550	-12.01%
Hard Liquor	VC/DVC	22,600	20,000	-2,600	-11.50%
Total Cost of Beverage Sold	VC/DVC	94,550	95,000	450	0.48%
Total COGS	**COGS**	807,137	825,000	17,863	2.21%
Gross Profit	**GP/CM**	1,498,973	1,655,000	156,027	10.41%
Operating Expenses (Costs)					
Wages (hourly)	VC/SVC	395,450	420,000	24,550	6.21%
Mandatory Benefits (hourly)	VC/SVC	71,182	75,600	4,418	6.21%
Hourly Payroll and Benefits	VC/SVC	466,632	495,600	28,968	6.21%
Direct Operating expenses	VC	142,309	150,000	7,691	5.40%
Marketing	VC	89,622	95,000	5,378	6.00%
Administrative & General	VC	66,000	70,000	4,000	6.06%
Total Operating expenses	VC	764,563	810,600	46,037	6.02%
Fixed Expenses, Overhead, Occupancy Cost					
Wages managerial	FXC	122,540	150,000	27,460	22.41%
Mandatory and other Benefits	FXC	26,959	33,000	6,041	22.41%
Energy & Utility services	FXC	121,000	125,000	4,000	3.31%
Rent/Interest	FXC	86,750	88,000	1,250	1.44%
Depreciation	FXC	80,496	83,000	2,504	3.11%
Total Fixed Expenses	FXC	437,745	479,000	41,255	9.42%
Profit, Net Income/Loss	P/NI/L	296,665	365,400	68,735	23.17%

Break Even Point Calculations

BEP for THIS year:		BEP for NEXT year:	
Sales:	2,306,110	Sales:	2,480,000
Variable Costs:	1,571,700	Variable Costs:	1,635,600
Fixed Costs:	437,745	Fixed Costs:	479,000
VR= (VC/S):	0.68153731	VR= (VC/S):	0.6595161
CR=(1-VR):	0.31846269	CR=(1-VR):	0.3404839
BEP (FXC/CR)	1,374,557	**BEP (FXC/CR)**	1,406,821

Purchasing, Receiving, Storing – simplified:

> The **"Theme"** and **"Concept"** of the establishment will lead to purchasing "Standards"
>
> The industry readily accepts the four "W's" of purchasing;
>
> **"WHY"** (need)
>
> **"WHAT"** (item)
>
> **"WHEN"** (date & time needed)
>
> **"WHERE"** (from)

Purchasing is based on standards specific to the individual establishment or chains. Every individual establishment is unique in their needs, hence they will have different standards based on their theme and concept. Just by looking at the different types of establishments, one can imagine the different fare being offered and the different products being procured.

"WHAT" Each of the illustrated food-service establishments have considerably different offerings on their menus and subsequently need different products to serve their customers needs and expectations.

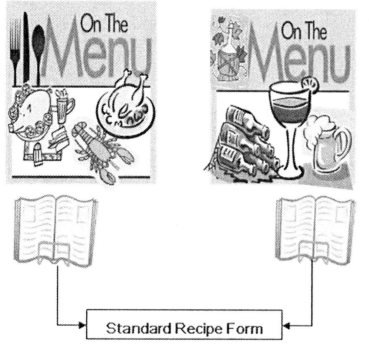

"WHY"

Because there is a **"Need"**. By offering Food and Beverage items on the respective menu(s), a justifiable need is created which allows procurement of these items.

From the two **"Bill of fare"** groups – Food and Beverage "Standard Recipes" are being created.

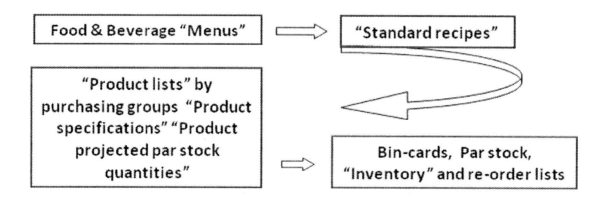

All offered menu items should be derived from cost extended standard recipes. **The products identified on these recipes need to have clearly defined standards of quality.**

This is achieved by completing a "Purchase Specification Form"

The purpose of a Product specification form is to document the expected standard for products based on all or some of the listed criteria. This form(s) may also be used, in a summary format, referred to as a market or call sheet sorted into the food-groups or potential suppliers for each food-group. Example; Rice would be Dry goods.

Sample:

Name or description of item: (example) Beef Rib-Eye – NAMP (National Association of Meat Purveyors), CMC (Canadian Meat Council) 112

Package – Size – dimensions: Insulated Card-board, N/A, N/A.

Weight – Volume – Count – Pieces: Four to a case, Vacuum packed 3.9 to 4.1 Kg each

Place of Origin: Canada or US

Grade – Canadian or equivalent: Canada AAA, USDA Choice

Quality description: Aged minimum 21 days, fresh, ripe, dry-aged...

Purchasing quantity: Two cases per week

Price per unit (expected): $10.50 per Kg

Rebate expected: 2% for COD and 2% for orders exceeding $1500.00 in four weeks

Value considerations/adjustments: N/A (This scenario applies in most cases to product prepared and/or packaged to your specification – such as dressings, marinades, condiments, toiletry, beverages. Due to the custom labelling/packaging there might be an up-charge which makes it necessary to consider its **value and potential benefit.**)

Product specification form				
Name:				
Brand name:				
Package - size- dimension:				
Weight - volume - count - pieces:				
Place of origin:				
Grade; Canadian - equivalent:				
Quality description:				
Additional Information:				
Purchasing quantity:				
Price per unit: (expected)				
Rebate: (expected) % or $				
Value considerations - adjustments:				
Send to Supplier:	A	B	C	D

"WHEN" and "WHERE"

The last two of the **"4 W'^s"** in purchasing refer to **TIME** and **WHERE** the product should be purchased from.

As less time there is to look for competitively priced items, based on purchase specifications, as more likely it is to pay a premium price for it. Worse, it may not be obtainable when needed.

The task to find reputable suppliers follows some established procedures which are being challenged by the availability of "One-stop-buying" for most of, if not all of your required products.

Note: On the bottom of the "Product specification form" there is a check-box for sending the "Spec" to Supplier A, B, C, D, for a price quotation. Once an answer is received it is recorded on a "Market" or "Call-sheet", aiding in the decision process of selecting specific suppliers for the type of comparable product. Most suppliers no longer participate in this rather time consuming method of quoting prices item for item separately, instead, they will supply you with their product list identifying the type, quality and cost of products they carry.

The established way of purchasing requires you to compare prices and other conditions from at least three different potential suppliers (vendors) based on your purchase specifications and to buy from two or more different suppliers.

Some advantages:

Ability to negotiate based on competitive offers. Selection of best supplier for specific products. Simplified credit/debit procedures. Personalized service from knowledgeable vendor representative.

Some disadvantages:

Frequency of different deliveries. Various credit arrangements. Considerable amount of time invested in ordering, tracking, receiving of products and monitoring of each vendors invoices due dates.

In comparison, One-stop-vendors may not provide a selection of different levels of quality products within one group of products. Due to the many varieties One-stop-vendors carry the representative may not have the intimate product knowledge you expect. Simplified accounting, one vendor – one credit arrangement- one invoice. Credit and debit procedures adhering to acceptable accounting principles involving considerable paper-work.

Both scenarios have obvious advantages and disadvantages – you must decide which is the most suitable method accommodating your needs.

The Purchasing Process

Needed products are identified by departments using Requisitions. These documents are forwarded to Stores/Purchasing office. They will be collated and sorted into Purchasing groups. Suppliers/Vendors are being selected by "Searching the market" using a "Market/Call" sheet, which contains the following info:

Product Category	Vendor "A"	Vendor "B"	Vendor "C"	Purchase from:
Product Name:	Co$t	Co$t	Co$t	A, B or C

The decision of who to buy from is NOT solely based on price: Other factors to be taken in consideration; Credit arrangements, Reputation of Supplier, Sanitary conditions, ability to deliver when needed, Accessibility, Discounts, Services (Sales-person, Computer software, Equipment)...

Upon selection of a Vendor, a P.O. (Purchase Order) with a unique number (unwritten contract) specified shipping instructions is issued to the Vendor.

All Purchase Order (P.O.) should bear a unique number. This number is issued by the Purchaser. By issuing a P.O.# you are entering into an un-written contract, which, in simple terms has the following meaning: The Vendor agrees; to fill the order "As ordered", based on the supplied purchase specifications and shipped within the stipulated time-frame. The authorized Purchaser agrees; to receive the shipped goods, provided that they are "As ordered" and will pay for them on time. A P.O.# may be issued with each individual order, or, as a "Blanket" order for a period of time with one specific supplier.

Upon receiving and examination of the ordered goods, the Invoice is compared to the P.O. for accuracy in quantity, quality and price of the items shipped. If everything is "As ordered" the Invoice is signed by the authorized receiver and the products are being directed to the appropriate areas. (Requisitioner – Storage – Production - Sales).

If there are discrepancies between the P.O. and Invoice, a Credit or Debit note, as appropriate, must be issued. (Accounting procedure)

A Credit note, issued by the Vendors representative (Driver) allows the Vendor to Credit your account with the value (Cost) of the returned goods.

A Debit note, issued by the Purchaser/Receiver allows the Vendor to Debit your account for goods which were shipped to you, but were not ordered by you or not on your invoice, but you decided to keep them.

All transactions (Date, time, Invoice #, P.O. #, Credit/Debit notes) are recorded on a **Receiving Summary Sheet**. This receiving summary sheet and all Invoice #, P.O. #, Credit/Debit notes are sent to the Accounting department for timely payment, and copies are being sent to Stores/Purchasing for reconciliation/control.

Helpful steps "prior" to selecting a Purveyor/Vendor:

- ✓ Check Vendors premises for sanitary standards
- ✓ Make a "Credit check" (especially when considering contract buying)
- ✓ Make reference calls
- ✓ Meet Sales representative – your first link to new products
- ✓ Discuss suitable credit arrangements
- ✓ Verify delivery conditions and frequency
- ✓ Specify conditions for substitutions of products
- ✓ Helpful steps "after" to selecting a purveyor:
- ✓ Monitor delivery terms and times
- ✓ Periodic "re-checking" of premises for sanitary standards
- ✓ Encourage visits of Sales representative – Samples - New products
- ✓ Establish list of persons with "ordering" authority to avoid duplicate orders
- ✓ Establish acceptable ordering methods; Issuance of P.O.#, telephone orders from identified authorized individuals only.
- ✓ Establish list of persons with "signing" authority for Invoices and "Debit notes"
- ✓ Do periodic checks to verify quality as specified and quantity as ordered
- ✓ Do periodic market price checks for price comparison with other suppliers

It is very important to establish a good relationship, built on trust, with your vendors/purveyors. Discrepancies such as short, or over shipments of orders can be resolve in an amicable fashion.

Common Purchasing methods:

"Call or Market Sheet" buying: as previously mentioned, refers to comparing quotations from "No less" than 3 potential suppliers.

"Blank cheque" buying refers to purchasing at any cost.

"Cost plus" buying refers to "the Vendors cost" plus other charges. Be fully aware what other charges could be before entering a deal. Example: If it says that the goods are **F.O.B.** Vancouver – it means the "freight on board" is paid for up to Vancouver, but shipping from Vancouver to your city, is your responsibility.

"Bidding – Open or Sealed" a formal method of buying – the Buyer invites several purveyors or the open market to quote prices (written) specific products. Bids are often placed on "Certain quantities, qualities, packaging, service and frequency", however, it is not uncommon to receive bids based solely on "Cost".

"Tender" or tendering is the process of making an offer on a bid. Offers may be conditional.

"Contract buying" often follows the bidding or tendering process and is formalized by a written agreement with very specific terms and payment conditions (up-front, throughout and at the end of the contract).

Receiving procedures:

Step one – compare invoice with Purchase order

Step two – Count number of boxes and part-boxes and/or weigh product

Step three – open boxes with knife and check content for: appropriate quantity, quality, freshness, signs of defrosting, dampness

Step four – if everything is OK sign invoice

Step five – if there are discrepancies, tape or tie open boxes for return and request a "Credit note" from driver clearly identifying the returned product type, quantity and cost, else, if extra product was shipped you wish to keep, issue a "Debit note" to the driver clearly identifying the retained product type, quantity and cost.

Step six – record delivery on the "Receiving summary sheet" as well as any Credit or Debit note.

Step seven – Load products on a platform-truck or similar device and distribute to the requisitioner or the appropriate storage area/facility (dry, refrigerated store or freezer)

Step eight – update bin cards

Bin Card					
Product Name:		Tomato paste			
A.P. Information: _Catelli_____			Product #: _00001_____		
Unit information: __1 cs = 12 x 2 ltr cans_____					
Date:	Quantity IN:	Cost:	Date:	Quantity OUT:	Balance:
01/01/XXXX	24	60.00			24
			02/01/XXXX	3	21
			03/01/XXXX	9	12
04/01/XXXX	12	30.00			24
			05/01/XXXX	15	9
Totals:	36	90.00	31/01/XXXX	27	9

Sample Perpetual Inventory Sheet

Product Name:	Product Code:	Period ending	Quantity IN: (From Bin Card)	Cost:	Date:	Quantity OUT:	Perpetual Inventory:	Actual Inventory:	Variance:	Extended Cost:
Tomato Paste		31/01/XXXX	36	90.00	31/01/XXXX	27	9	8	-1	20.00
Totals:			36.00	90.00		27.00	9.00	8.00	-1.00	20.00

there are no specific guidelines, it is the writers opinion to have a minimum of two days of perishable goods on hand prior to the next delivery. Dry goods are usually less fragile and subsequently bought in larger quantities and should be on a separate par-stock list.

A functional option in addition to the Perpetual inventory is a "Par-stock - Purchasing - Re-order add-on" with an estimated cost calculator built-in.

Purchasing:

Par Stock:	Re-Order Quantity:	Cost of Re-Order:
20	12	30.00

Physical Inventory Sheet:

Inventory Sheet	Inventory area:						
Taken by:	Date:		Extended by:		Date:		
						Order up to Par-stock	
ITEM-BRAND DESCRIPTION	Item Weight/Size Count/Vol.	Unit Size Count	Unit #'s in Stock	Cost per Unit	Inventory Extended Cost $	Par Stock	Re-order #'s Units
Tomato Paste	Case/ 12/ 2L	1 x 2L	8	2.50	20.00	20	12
					0.00		0
					0.00		0
					0.00		0
					0.00		0
					0.00		0
					0.00		0
					0.00		0
					0.00		0
					0.00		0
Number of items in Inventory:			8				
				Value of Inventory $:	20.00		

Don't just count your inventory – Control it...

FIFO – First In First Out – rules – Label food products with the receiving date, expiry date, and proper (usage) description. Inventory, simply put, is the quantity of goods "On hand". In the food service business, we purchase raw foods, products, and materials, convert them into menu-able products for our guests, and, hopefully, produce profits for our operation in the process. To be a successful Chef, Food and Beverage manager, or Kitchen manager you need to positively impact profitability by controlling Product and Labour Cost.

Inventory for Profit...

Basic inventory management procedures centre around having just enough of what is needed (given period of time) and limiting waste, thereby maximizing profits.

Taking inventory...

For maximum control, daily, alternatively, weekly, monthly, quarterly. By law, in order to produce an Income statement, inventory needs to be taken once a year. Although daily inventory is labour intensive, if it is narrowed down to costly items it will provide important data. Apparent theft, inappropriate handling, spoilage and breakage can be reacted to in a timely fashion. Once a week, or month has gone by, it is almost impossible to find out what caused shortages. Inventory items need to be assessed for validity – item removed from menu, yet still in inventory...

A commonly used inventory method is the A, B, C method.

A	B	C
Daily/Weekly	**Weekly/Monthly**	**Monthly/Quarterly**
High Value, easily transportable as well as perishable. Re-order on an as-needed basis only.	Lesser Value than A. Expiry date (aroma, freshness, temperature, humidity) sensitive.	Least Costly, Not perishable, Common ingredient, large quantity-discount purchasing.

Managing your business utilizing inventory information by preparing a simple internal income statement (see page 8)

Revenue minus C.O.G.S. (O.I. + P. – C.I.) = G.P. or C.M.

Revenue minus C.O.G.S. (Cost of Goods Sold) equals Gross Profit or CM Contribution Margin.

(in this case Actual Food or Beverage Cost %) compared to Projected Cost % will allow you to detect differences (variances) and subsequently provide you with maximum control.

Many businesses utilize computer software P.O.S. (Point of Sales Systems) connected to an Inventory System providing a great variety of reports at will. In order to calculate the C.O.G.S. one must know the Value of the O.I. (Opening Inventory) and the C.I. (Closing Inventory) and the Purchases.

To complete the Purchasing, Receiving, Storing – simplified section, the method of Inventory Turn-Over must be mentioned.

Usually it is the Chef's and/or Managers responsibility to ensure that there is sufficient product on hand to operate for a determined period of time. Insufficient stock and stockpiling could lead to problems, such as: Increased food cost due to spoilage, expired /stale dated product, excessive amounts of money tied up in products for sale, labour cost in moving inventory around, increased opportunity for theft and possibly accident causing due to tight space.

A common technique used in establishing and monitoring inventory adequacy is to calculate how often inventory items have been purchased within an accounting period (usually one month). This purchasing frequency will depend on many factors such as inventory space, market price of products and available cash to be tied-up in storage.

To measure how frequently inventory has been consumed (used-up) and re-stocked during an accounting period, management uses a Inventory turnover calculation method:, also referred to as Rate of inventory turnover.

Firstly it must be acknowledged that not all products purchased are intended to turn-over within one accounting period. Perishables should be turned over considerably more often while product s which improve with age such as some wines may be kept purposely for an extended period of time.

Formulae:

Inventory Rate:

Average Inventory = Opening Inventory + Closing Inventory

divided by 2 = average

Inventory turn-over = Product Cost (Food cost)

divided by Average Inventory

> **Example:**
>
> Opening Inventory: $7,655.00
>
> Closing Inventory: $7,775.00
>
> Food cost: $18,500.00
>
> Average Inventory calculation = 7,655 + 7,775 = 15,430
>
> divided by 2 = **7,715**
>
> Inventory turnover calculation = 18,500 (Food cost)
>
> divided by 7,715 = **2.398 or 2.4**

In the example, provided the inventory rate is consistently 2.4 the inventory rate for the year will be 28.8 times, or once every 1.806 weeks. Most establishments consider inventory sufficient if it last for one to two weeks – using two weeks as a guide-line the provided example is slightly less than the guide-line.

Product Inventory extended cost calculations:

As previously mentioned, every company must report the value of their inventory at least once a year. Product inventory is a "Short term asset" and is listed on a "Balance Sheet" in the group of Assets.

There are five methods of calculating the value of the inventory; You may select any one of them, but you may not select more than one method for one operating period (maximum one year).

L.P.P. (Last Purchase Price cost approach)

In this method it is assumed that the "Last invoiced" price is the price you paid throughout the reporting period. This method is the easiest of the four methods and commonly used by small businesses since invoices don't need to be researched. This method is often mistaken with the LIFO approach.

L.I.F.O. (Last in first out cost approach)

In this method the purchase price from the Opening Inventory and subsequent purchases during the inventory period, up to number of inventory items, is used to calculate the value of the inventory. This method is used, if applicable, to utilize the lowest purchase cost to deflate the value of the inventory, increasing the Cost of Goods Sold and subsequently reducing net income.

F.I.F.O. (First in First out – average of last purchases)

In this method the cost of the remaining purchases during the inventory period is divided by the number of units bought and the resulting average unit cost is multiplied with the number of units in stock.

Weighted AVERAGE cost approach

In this method the cost of all purchases during the inventory period plus the cost of the Opening Inventory is divided by the number of units bought and the units from the opening inventory. The resulting average unit cost is multiplied with the number of units in stock. Because of its complexity and accuracy this method is the basis of commonly used computer inventory programs.

ACTUAL cost approach

In this method the unit cost of each purchase during the inventory period is multiplied by the number of remaining units from each period. See example on next page. This method works well if the product has been marked with cost price stickers (Unit times unit cost)

I suggest you consult your accountant before implementing any of the above methods.

See next page for examples...

Blank space for notes:

Pickles DEMO Workshop

Calculate the $ Value of the Inventory based on the following info:

Purchased item: Dill Pickles (1 pail = 16 litre)
Purchase Dates and Quantities and Costs:

	Par stock	8	16 L pails			

	Date:	Quantity	Case/Cost	Ext.Cost	Perpetual	
O.I.	Jan 31st	8	21.00	168.00	8	8
Issued	Feb 1st	2	0.00	0.00	-2	6
Purch	Feb 3rd	2	21.50	43.00	2	8
Issued	Feb 3rd	3	0.00	0.00	-3	5
Purch	Feb 7th	4	21.00	84.00	4	9
Issued	Feb 9th	6	0.00	0.00	-6	3
Purch	Feb 14th	5	20.50	102.50	5	8
Total Purchases only:		11	63.00	229.50		
Total including O.I.:		19	84.00	397.50		

Case Cost As Purchased	1	21.00	20.86

C.C.A.P. plus Opening Inv.	1	21.00	20.92

On February 15th Inventory is taken — **8** pails are in stock

What is the Total $ Value of the Inventory using the....

ACTUAL Cost approach:	L.I.F.O. Cost approach:	F.I.F.O. Cost approach:
(Actual Cost of available stock as purchased)	(Cost of O.I. and subsequent purchases up to corresponding # of units in inventory)	(Average of available stock as purchased)
165.50	**168.00**	**165.78**

L.P.P. Cost approach:	Weighted AVERAGE Cost approach:
(Last Cost as purchased is used for calculation)	(Average of all purchases + O.I.)
164.00	**167.37**

The "Break-even-point" simplified *transcribed by Klaus Theyer C.C.C.*

Based on the book "Principles of Food, Beverage, and Labour Cost Controls" – sixth edition, by Paul R. Dittmer and Gerald G. Griffin. Published by John Wiley & Sons, Inc. ISBN 0-471-29325-3

The Break Even Point (Part 1)

In order to calculate a "Break even point" (where sales cover all costs, but no profit is made) you should be familiar with the following commonly used abbreviations and terminology:

S = SALES and/or REVENUE

Revenue refers to all Sales earned in exchange for Goods and Services (not including Taxes - as Taxes are NOT Revenue)

VC = VARIABLE COST

referring to "All Costs which **are** changing with Sales volume"

VR = VARIABLE RATE - Equation VR = (VC ÷ S)

This Rate is calculated by dividing VARIABLE COST'S by SALES

CR = CONTRIBUTION RATE - Equation CR = (1 - VR)

Contribution Rate is a dividing factor and is established by either taking the whole number " 1 " and subtracting the Variable Rate expressed in a whole number (or fraction thereof) or replacing the number "1" with 100 % and subtracting the Variable Rate in a percentage number. Either - or is correct - however **DO NOT** mix the two methods.

FXC = FIXED COST

referring to "All Costs which **do not** change with Sales volume" (For the purpose of BEP calculations, Labour cost is usually considered a Fixed Cost)

CM = CONTRIBUTION MARGIN - Equation CM = (S - VC)

Is the Dollar Amount remaining after subtracting the Variable Cost of an item from its sales price.

P = PROFIT - Equation P = (S - VC - SVC - FXC)

Profit refers to "Revenue minus Variable, Semi-Variable and Fixed Costs.

BEP = THE BREAK EVEN POINT is calculated by dividing the Fixed Cost with the Contribution Rate:

BEP = FXC   (Fixed Cost)
         CR   (Contribution Rate)

To establish what Sales are needed to earn a desired amount of Profit, the formula should read:

Formula # 1   S = **FXC (Fixed Costs) + P (Profit expectations)**
                          CR (Contribution Rate)

More useful formulas:

Formula # 2	Formula # 3	Formula # 4
CR = **FXC + P** S	P = (S x CR) – FXC	FXC = (S x CR) – P

The Break Even Point (Part 2)

U = UNIT

Singular or smallest (dividable) part of re-sellable (production items)

Individual unit sales data is needed in order to calculate the breakeven point.

PSTS = PROPORTIONAL SHARE OF TOTAL SALES

Ratio of Unit sales in comparison to Total Unit Sales within a given time period or/also the Ratio of Dollar sales in comparison to Total Dollar Sales within a given time period.

AVERAGE SALES OR COVER

The result of dividing total dollar sales for a period by the number of customers served in that period; an average dollar figure representing the average amount spent by customers.

AVERAGE VARIABLE COST

The result of dividing total variable cost for a period by the number of customers served in that period.

AVERAGE CONTRIBUTION MARGIN

The dollar difference between average sales and average variable cost; the dollar amount remaining after average Variable Cost is subtracted from the average Sale.

AVERAGE VARIABLE RATE

The ratio of average variable cost to average sale, normally expressed in decimal form.

UNIT SALES REQUIRED TO BREAK EVEN

The number of average sales required to achieve break even volume.

COST/VOLUME/PROFIT RATIO ANALYSIS.

It is important to understand that in order to attempt a cost-volume-profit analysis, reasonable accurate data of the following is available:

1. Costs can be classified as Fixed or Variable, with reasonable accuracy.

NOTE: In any calculation involving Units, Variable and/or Semi-Variable Costs - as allocated on a profit and loss statement, usually are Fixed Cost in a Break Even Point calculation.

2. Variable Costs are clearly related to Business volume. As Business increases, Variable Cost will increase; as volume decreases - Variable Cost should decrease, too. As an obvious example of Variable Costs are; Food, Beverage, (Directly Variable), and Labour Cost (Semi Variable or Fixed Cost).

3. Fixed Costs are relatively stable and will remain so within the Relevant Range.

4. Sales Prices will remain constant for the Period covered by the analysis.

5. The Sales Mix in the Establishment will remain relatively constant.

To find Answers to Questions such as:

What Profit will an Establishment Earn at a given Sales Level?

How many Sales (or Covers) will be required to earn a given Profit?

How many Sales (or Covers) will be required to reach the Break Even Point?

You may split these questions into two categories;

1. Those which can be solved with Dollar ($) formulas
2. Those which can be solved with Unit (U) formulas.

These formulas have useful applications. If the Fixed Costs and the anticipated Sales level are known, and a target Profit has been decided, it is relative easy to calculate the Variable Rate;

Fixed Costs 160,000.00, **Sales Potential** 500,000.00, **Profit Target** 40,000.00

Using (Formula #2) we can determine a projected C.R.

F.C. 160,000 + 40,000

S 500,000 = C.R. of .4

Since C.R. = 1. - V.R., then V.R. must be .6, meaning Variable Cost may not exceed 60% of the expected Sales, or in other words $00.60 out of every dollar Sales is the maximum that can be used to cover Variable Costs.

Using selected figures from above, and (Formula #3) lets verify the Profit potential.

(S 500,000. x C.R. .4) - F.C. 160,000. = P = 40,000

U.S.R. =   FXC $30,000

           C.M. per Unit or $10.00 = 3,000 (USR)

As previously calculated (stated) the Average Sales Price per Unit is $16.00 the Break Even Point would occur at $48,000. Dollar Sales. (3,000. Units x $16.00).

Calculating Average Variable Rate.

In the previous example the focus was on the BE point for one Item. Realistically, there are very few Establishments which carry one item only. Therefore it is necessary to allow for the variation in Cost and Selling Price of the different items offered.

This is done by calculating all Variable Costs - Sales - and subsequently the Variable Rates. See example.

	Unit V.C.	S Price	Unit V.R.	Totals Sold	$ V.C.	$ S
Steak	10.00	16.00	.625	10	100.00	160.00
Scallops	6.00	12.00	.5	10	60.00	120.00
Chicken	4.00	10.00	.4	10	40.00	100.00
Spaghetti	2.00	8.00	.25	10	20.00	80.00
				40	220.00.	460.00

Since V.R. equals V.C. ÷ Sales the Result is:

Units Sold	40
V.C. in $	220.00.
Sales $	460.00

$$A.V.R. = \frac{220.00 \text{ V.C.}}{460.00 \text{ S}} = .478$$

Assuming that Total Fixed Cost was $64,328 then BE point would be:

$$BE = \frac{64,328 \text{ FXC}}{C.R. (1. - .478)} = \$123,233.72$$

The average cheque amounts to $11.50, therefore, 10,716 meals must be sold to Break Even. ($123,233.72 divided by $11.50 = 10,716)

Happy cooking

MENU ANALYSIS – MENU ENGINEERING:

The basis of the menu analysis technique described below was developed some years ago by **Michael L. Kasavana and Donald I. Smith** and was described in a book they published in 1982.* Known as menu engineering, the technique is now widely known and respected and has been the subject of numerous papers and articles. ***Michael L. Kasavana and Donald I. Smith,** *Menu Engineering-A Practical Guide to Menu Analysis* (Lansing, Michigan: Hospitality Publications, 1982).

Modified to conform to the attached sample worksheet for the benefit of studious Culinarians, by Klaus Theyer C.C.C.

Although some do not agree with all the conclusions drawn by Kasavana and Smith, their approach to menu analysis is both interesting and revealing. This book does not fully expose their method, which can best be obtained from their book. It would be good practice to investigate the various methods of menu analysis available today and select a method which is best suited.

Since Michael L. Kasavana and Donald I. Smith introduced their method of Menu Analysis and Menu Engineering to the industry, other analytical methods have been pioneered and adapted, however, the principal reason for performing a Menu Analysis has not changed: To determine which menu item performs satisfactorily by being popular with the customers and subsequently is a "Good Seller" yet producing the expected amount of "Contribution – Gross Profit" in comparison to all other offered menu items.

When performing a menu analysis it is very important to categorize menu items to be evaluated, by meal periods as offered; Breakfast, Lunch, Afternoon Tea, Dinner, as well as by types of offerings such as main courses (with possible sub-categories such as Pasta and Pizza dishes, Fish, Shellfish, Meats, Poultry, Game, Specials, House speciality or ethnic origin items, Health food and/or dietary choices and Vegetarian/Vegan offerings), Appetizers, Soups, Salads, Sandwiches and Desserts. This list can be expanded or reduced to suit any establishment.

This method of analysis can be applied to any type of menu such as; beverage, hot – cold, alcoholic and non-alcoholic, take-out, catering, banquet and special occasions, cycle (cyclical) menus, a la carte, table d'hôte, du jour, market and California type menu.

In order to perform a menu analysis it is essential to work with accurate data. Although a full menu analysis is quite labour intensive, it does provide a means for monitoring the effectiveness of offerings to maximize profits. Additionally, it provides some general insights that are useful for potentially increasing the profitability of a menu.

A example of a menu engineering worksheet based on one group of menu offerings from an a la carte menu is illustrated **on page 75.** In order to fully understand and utilise the example on page 75, one must understand the meaning of the method and the calculated results. Once this information is evaluated a proposal for changes can be made and implemented.

Three examples are provided with a second illustration of the spreadsheet from page 75 showing the result of possible changes.

The following columns (in brackets) contain the necessary information used in this menu engineering worksheet:

- A. *Numbering of each menu item to calculate total offerings and to calculate averages*
- B. *Menu items described and categorized (from menu)*
- C. *Number of menu items sold (from sales record – POS)*
- D. *Calculation of Menu item sales mix percentage also referred to as Menu mix or Popularity Index (Individual item sold divided by total of items sold X 100)*
- E. *Individual item Food/Beverage cost (from Standard recipe)*
- F. *Menu item Selling price (from menu)*
- G. *Individual item Contribution Margin/Gross profit (F – E)*
- H. *Total item cost based on number of items sold (C X E)*
- I. *Menu item Sales/Revenue (F X C)*
- J. *Sold menu item Contribution margin or Gross profit (I – H)*
- K. *Result of classification based on calculation from Line 24*
- L. *Result of classification based on calculation from Line 25*
- M. *Result of classification based on calculation from Line 28 to 31*

Column D: Menu Mix Percent

The menu mix percent for each item is calculated by dividing the number of units sold by the total number of units sold for all items. For example, Lobster bisque accounted for 32 portions out of the total portion sales for all items: 181.

The menu mix percent for this item is calculated as follows.

$$\frac{32}{181} = .1768, \text{ or } 17.68\,\%$$

The menu mix percent for each of the other items is calculated in the same way.

Column G: Item CM

The Item Contribution Margin is the amount available from each sale to contribute toward meeting all other costs of operation and, when those costs have been met, to provide profit. (CM) is defined as **sales price minus variable cost per unit**. For simplicity reasons and for purposes of this analysis, product cost is treated as the **only** variable cost. **Therefore, the CM for Lobster bisque is determined by subtracting the portion cost for the item from its sales price, as follows.**

Sales Price	$4.50
- Food Cost	$3.05
= CM	$1.45

Column J: Menu CM

The menu contribution margin is calculated by multiplying the number of unit sold for each menu item by its contribution margin. Thus, for Lobster bisque,

32 Units Sold x $1.45 CM = **$46.40 Menu CM**

Editors Note: Alternatively, CM may be calculated by subtracting Menu Cost *(Column H)* from Menu Sales *(Column I)* This calculation indicates the total of contribution margins provided by the particular menu item.

The sum of all the individual totals is **found in Box Q.**

Box S (In column G)

The figure in **Box S** is the average contribution margin, determined by dividing the total in **Box Q** by the total number of units sold, found in **Box N**. For the illustrated worksheet the calculation is:

$$\frac{\$490.31 \text{ Total CM (Box Q)}}{181 \text{ Units Sold (Box N)}} = \$2.71$$

Box T (in columns H to K)

The figure in **Box T** requires careful consideration. **This is the percentage of an entire menu represented by each item on that menu, multiplied by 70 percent.***

*****This is a figure established by Kasavana and Smith and based wholly on their own experience. They state that 70 percent produces the most useful analysis.**

There are ten items on the menu, each is one-tenth, or 10 percent, of the menu. Similarly, if there were five items on the menu, each would be one-fifth, or 20 percent, of

the total. The figure in **Box T** is calculated by dividing one menu item by the total number of items and then **multiplying the result by .7 (70 percent).**
Thus,

$$\frac{1 \times .7}{10} = .07, \text{ or } 7.0\%$$

This figure will be used when making entries in **Column L**, as discussed below.

Column K: CM Category

The entries in this column, **L for "Low" and H for "High,** are made after comparing the contribution margin for each menu item *(Column F)* with the average contribution margin for the menu **(Box S)**. If the contribution margin for a given menu item is lower than the average contribution margin, the entry for that item in **Column K is "L" for low.** If the contribution margin is higher than average, the entry is **"H" for high.** For example, the contribution margin for Lobster bisque is $1.45, which is considerably lower than the average contribution margin for the menu, $2.71. Thus, the entry for that item in Column is an **"L" for low.**

Column L: MM Category

The entries in **Column L** (L and H for "Low" and "High') are determined by comparing the menu mix percentage for each item in **Column C** with the figure in **Box T**. For example, the menu mix percentage for Lobster bisque is 17.68 percent. Compared to **the 7.0 percent figure in Box T, this is high**, so the entry for Lobster bisque is the letter **H**. The menu mix percentage for Lady Curzon is 3.31 percent and, because this is **lower than the 7.0 percent in Box T**, the letter **L** has been entered.

Because all entries in **Column K and Column L** must be one of two letters (either H or L), there are four possible combination of letters: **H / H, L / L, H / L, & L / H**. These four possible combinations are used to identify menu items and, in the unique language of menu engineering, each has been given a name:

H | H is a Star. A Star is a menu item that produces both high contribution margin and high volume. These are the items that foodservice operators would prefer to sell.

L | L is a Dog. A Dog is a menu item that produces a comparatively low contribution margin and accounts for relatively low volume. These are probably the least desirable items to have on a menu.

Editors note: This scenario often applies to Clubs and Ethnic establishments which cater to a specific audience who directly or indirectly demand the menu offering.

L | H is a Plowhorse. A Plowhorse is a menu item that produces a low contribution margin, but accounts for relatively high volume. These are items that are popular with customers but contribute comparatively little profit per unit sold.

H | L is a Puzzle. A Puzzle is a menu item that produces a high contribution margin, but accounts for comparatively low sales volume.

Editors note: This scenario can be found in Clubs and Ethnic establishments which cater to a specific audience who directly or indirectly demand the menu offering.

Once the worksheet is completed and results are analysed, the establishment may use different approaches, as described below and then determine the changes, if any, that would improve the menu. An illustrated example is provided on page 76.

Dogs: Because dogs are both unprofitable and unpopular, they should be removed from the menu and replaced with more profitable items unless (a) there is a valid reason for continuing to sell a dog (as with an item that promotes other sales) or (b) its profitability can somehow be increased to an acceptable level. This will require changes to the item in some way. One way of changing an item from a dog to a puzzle is to increase contribution margin per unit, which might be done by increasing the sales price.

Plowhorse: Plowhorses are popular, but relatively unprofitable. This/these item(s) should be kept on the menu, but attempts should be made to increase their contribution margins without decreasing volume. One possibility would be to decrease standard portion size slightly and at the same time improve the appearance of the product.

Puzzles: Puzzles are comparatively profitable, but relatively unpopular. They should be kept on the menu, but attempts should be made to increase their popularity without substantially decreasing their profitability. There are any number of ways to do this, including repositioning items to more favourable locations on the menu, featuring items as specials suggested to diners by servers, and/or changing appearances or menu descriptions of these items to increase their appeal.

Stars: Stars are both profitable and popular and should normally be left alone, unless there is some valid reason for change. Because of the popularity of Stars, it is sometimes possible to increase their menu prices without affecting volume, thus increasing their profitability.

Scenarios of possible changes:

1. **Lady Curzon,** was replaced with Minestra, an item with a higher contribution margin ($1.25 lower Cost). While sales volume did not change, the higher contribution margin changed the classification of the item from Dog to Puzzle. In addition, total revenues, total contribution margin, and average contribution margin were all increased.

2. **Tomato Shrimp,** a Plowhorse, **the Selling Price was increased in price by $1.50**. Volume was not affected because of the popularity of the item, its relatively low sales price, and the minimal price increase. While the item remains a Plowhorse, total revenues, total contribution margin and average contribution margin were all increased.

3. **Consommé Celestine,** a Puzzle, was repositioned on the menu and suggested to customers by servers. **This resulted in an increase in sales volume**, reclassifying the item from Puzzle to Star. This change had some negative impact on the sales of the Chicken Bouillon, although the Bouillon remains a Star. However the higher contribution margin and higher sales price for the Consommé Celestine, compared to the Chicken Bouillon, produced an overall increase in total revenue, total contribution margin and average contribution margin. Thus the net effect was desirable.

Following this exercise, Management decided to abandon their policy of **One –Price-Selling-Price** for this category of menu items and to gradually adjust Cost and Selling Prices to obtain a satisfactory Cost Percentage and Gross Profit Margin closely monitoring Customers reaction. **A review of the results on page 77 indicates that there are now 3 Dogs to be dealt with, caused by low popularity of these items.** It cannot be emphasized often enough to frequently complete a Menu Analysis to track changes in patterns and to make necessary adjustments as quickly as possible. The effects described above and illustrated on pages 75 to 77 show clearly the value of menu engineering as an analytical tool that can be used for many purposes.

Menu Analysis ~ Menu engineering method developed by Michael L. Kasavana & Donald I. Smith, published in 1982.
Transcribed and presented by Klaus Theyer C.C.C.   Template for Student use only.   File name: 10itemsA

	A	B	C	D	E	F	G	H	I	J	K	L	M
4		File name: 10itemsA	Menu	MenuMix	Item Food	Item Sales	Item Cont.	MenuCost	MenuSales	Menu CM	CM	MM	MenuItem Classifi-
5	#		Items	SalesMix	Item Food	Price	Margin	C.O.G.S.	Items Rev.	M.C.M.	Category	Category	-ication
6	of	(Formulas) ==>	# Sold	Pop.Index	Cost	I.S.P.	I.C.M.				L:H	L:H	S:D:P:P
7	items	Menu Item - Category:	MM	MM %	I.F.C.	S.P.	(F - E)	(E x C)	(F x C)	(1 - H)			
8	1	SOUPS: Tomato Basil	15	8.29%	0.68	4.50	3.82	10.20	67.50	57.30	H	H	Star
9	1	Tomato Shrimp	27	14.92%	2.85	4.50	1.65	76.95	121.50	44.55	L	H	Plowhorse
10	1	Pot Likker	22	12.15%	0.83	4.50	3.67	18.26	99.00	80.74	H	H	Star
11	1	Mushroom Consomme	12	6.63%	1.58	4.50	2.92	18.96	54.00	35.04	H	L	Puzzle
12	1	Navy Bean	9	4.97%	0.98	4.50	3.52	8.82	40.50	31.68	H	L	Puzzle
13	1	Chicken bouillon	24	13.26%	0.75	4.50	3.75	18.00	108.00	90.00	H	H	Star
14	1	Lobster bisque	32	17.68%	3.05	4.50	1.45	97.60	144.00	46.40	L	H	Plowhorse
15	1	Liverdumpling soup	22	12.15%	1.90	4.50	2.60	41.80	99.00	57.20	L	H	Plowhorse
16	1	Consomme Celestine	12	6.63%	1.05	4.50	3.45	12.60	54.00	41.40	H	L	Puzzle
17	1	Lady Curzon	6	3.31%	3.50	4.50	1.00	21.00	27.00	6.00	L	L	Dog
18	10	<== Totals ==>	181	100%	17.17	45.00	27.83	324.19	814.50	490.31			

	N	O	P	Q	R	S	T	
20	# of	Tot. of H	Tot. of I	= P - O	= O ÷ P	= Q ÷ N	(1÷ no. of Items x .7) or (1÷ no. of Items x 70%)	
21	items							
22	10	324.19	814.50	490.31	39.80%	2.71	(1÷10 x .7) = 7.00%	

24	For Column K: (H:L)	Compare G for each item with S. If lower than S then L, if higher than S then H.			
25	For Column L: (H:L)	Compare MM% for each item with T. If lower than T then L, if higher than T then H.			

		Column	K	L	
27	Scenario:				
28	combination of		H	H	equals = **Star**
29	combination of		L	L	equals = **Dog**
30	combination of		L	H	equals = **Plowhorse**
31	combination of		H	L	equals = **Puzzle**

	A	B	C	D	E	F	G	H	I	J	K	L	M
1		Menu Analysis ~ Menu engineering method developed by Michael L. Kasavana & Donald I. Smith, published in 1982.											
2		Revised Analysis following applied changes as mentioned on page 74											
3		Transcribed and presented by Klaus Theyer C.C.C. Template for Student use only.											
4		File name: 10itemsA	Menu	MenuMix	Item Food	Item Sales	Item Cont.						MenuItem
5	#		Items	SalesMix	Cost	Price	Margin	MenuCost	MenuSales	Menu CM	CM	MM	Classifi-
6	of	(Formulas) ==>	# Sold	Pop.Index	I.F.C.	I.S.P.	I.C.M.	C.O.G.S.	Items Rev.	M.C.M.	Category	Category	-ication
7	items	Menu Item - Category:	MM	MM %		S.P.	(F - E)	(E x C)	(F x C)	(I - H)	L : H	L : H	S:D:P:P
8	1	SOUPS: Tomato Basil	15	8.15%	0.68	4.50	3.82	10.20	67.50	57.30	H	H	Star
9	1	Tomato Shrimp	27	14.67%	2.35	5.50	3.15	63.45	148.50	85.05	H	H	Star
10	1	Pot Likker	22	11.96%	0.83	4.50	3.67	18.26	99.00	80.74	H	H	Star
11	1	Mushroom Consomme	12	6.52%	1.58	4.50	2.92	18.96	54.00	35.04	L	L	Dog
12	1	Navy Bean	9	4.89%	0.98	4.50	3.52	8.82	40.50	31.68	H	L	Puzzle
13	1	Chicken bouillon	24	13.04%	0.75	4.50	3.75	18.00	108.00	90.00	H	H	Star
14	1	Lobster bisque	32	17.39%	3.05	4.50	1.45	97.60	144.00	46.40	L	H	Plowhorse
15	1	Liverdumpling soup	22	11.96%	1.90	4.50	2.60	41.80	99.00	57.20	L	H	Plowhorse
16	1	Consomme Celestine	15	8.15%	1.05	4.50	3.45	15.75	67.50	51.75	H	H	Star
17	1	Minestra	6	3.26%	1.25	4.50	3.25	7.50	27.00	19.50	H	L	Puzzle
18	10	<== Totals ==>	184	100%	14.42	46.00	31.58	300.34	855.00	554.66			
19													
20	# of	N	O	P	Q	R	S	T					
21	items	Tot. of C	Tot. of H	Tot. of I	= P - O	= O ÷ P	= Q ÷ N	(1 ÷ no. of Items x .7) or (1 ÷ no. of Items x 70%)					
22	10	184	300.34	855.00	554.66	35.13%	3.01	(1÷10 x .7) = 7.00%					
23													
24		For Column K: (H:L)	Compare G for each item with S. If lower than S then L, if higher than S then H.										
25		For Column L: (H:L)	Compare MM% for each item with T. If lower than T then L, if higher than T then H.										
26					Column	K	L						
27		Scenario:				K	L						
28		combination of				H	H	equals =	Star				
29		combination of				L	L	equals =	Dog				
30		combination of				L	H	equals =	Plowhorse				
31		combination of				H	L	equals =	Puzzle				

	A	B	C	D	E	F	G	H	I	J	K	L	M	N
2		Revised Analysis following applied Selling Price changes as mentioned on page 74												
3		Transcribed and presented by Klaus Theyer C.C.C.					Template for Student use only.							
4		File name: 10itemsA												
5	#		Menu Items	MenuMix SalesMix	Item Food Cost	Item Sales Price I.S.P.	Item Cont. Margin I.C.M.	MenuCost C.O.G.S.	MenuSales Items Rev.	Menu CM M.C.M.	CM Category	MM Category	MenuItem Classifi- ication	Product Cost
6	of	(Formulas) ==>	# Sold	Pop.Index	I.F.C.	S.P.	(F - E)	(E x C)	(F x C)	(I - H)	L : H	L : H	S:D:P:P	Percentage
7	items	Menu Item - Category:	MM	MM %										
8	1	SOUPS: Tomato Basil	15	8.15%	0.68	4.50	3.82	10.20	67.50	57.30	L	H	Plowhorse	15.11%
9	1	Tomato Shrimp	27	14.67%	2.35	7.00	4.65	63.45	189.00	125.55	H	H	Star	33.57%
10	1	Pot Likker	22	11.96%	0.83	4.50	3.67	18.26	99.00	80.74	L	H	Plowhorse	18.44%
11	1	Mushroom Consomme	12	6.52%	1.58	5.50	3.92	18.96	66.00	47.04	L	L	Dog	28.73%
12	1	Navy Bean	9	4.89%	0.98	4.50	3.52	8.82	40.50	31.68	L	L	Dog	21.78%
13	1	Chicken bouillon	24	13.04%	0.75	4.50	3.75	18.00	108.00	90.00	L	H	Plowhorse	16.67%
14	1	Lobster bisque	32	17.39%	3.05	7.50	4.45	97.60	240.00	142.40	H	H	Star	40.67%
15	1	Liverdumpling soup	22	11.96%	1.90	6.50	4.60	41.80	143.00	101.20	H	H	Star	29.23%
16	1	Consomme Celestine	15	8.15%	1.05	4.50	3.45	15.75	67.50	51.75	L	H	Plowhorse	23.33%
17	1	Minestra	6	3.26%	1.25	4.50	3.25	7.50	27.00	19.50	L	L	Dog	27.78%
18	10	<== Totals ==>	184	100%	14.42	53.50	39.08	300.34	1047.50	747.16				26.95%
19														
20	# of	N	O	P	Q	R	S	T						
21	items	Tot. of C	Tot. of H	Tot. of I	= P - O	= O ÷ P	= Q ÷ N	(1÷ no. of Items x .7) or (1÷ no. of Items x 70%)						
22	10	184	300.34	1047.50	747.16	28.67%	4.06	(1÷10 x .7) = 7.00%						
23														
24		For Column K: (H:L)	Compare G for each item with S. If lower than S then L, if higher than S then H.											
25		For Column L: (H:L)	Compare MM% for each item with T. If lower than T then L, if higher than T then H.											
26			Column											
27		Scenario:	K	L										
28		combination of	H	H	equals =	Star								
29		combination of	L	L	equals =	Dog								
30		combination of	L	H	equals =	Plowhorse								
31		combination of	H	L	equals =	Puzzle								

A Chef's Companion to Cost Control

Although a full Menu Analysis as previously described and illustrated is an excellent method of evaluating Menu items, by group, periodically. For a daily quick analysis attention must be given to Popularity of items and to the Sales Mix (Menu Mix). Recipe and Selling prices have been calculated to satisfy the "Desired and/or Ideal cost" yet, in order to offer items on a menu in a group such as Appetizers, Soups, Main courses, Desserts, Beverages with a uniform Selling price (i.e. all soups are sold for $7.50) it is unavoidable to have a fluctuation in Cost percentages. The ideal situation is to sell the items with the lowest cost more often than items with a higher cost and subsequently achieve a higher Gross profit margin compared to each item selling in equal number of units.

See the two examples below:

	A	B	C	D	E	F	G	H	I	J	K	L
1	Simple Menu Analysis		Sales					Recipe or		Item	Total	
2	by Klaus Theyer C.C.C.		Menu Mix		COGS	Menu	Revenue	Project.	Actual	GP or CM	Sold Item	Contrib.
3			Popularity		Total	Price	Total	Product	Product	Contrib.	Contrib.	Margin
4	Menu Item:		Index %	Item	Cost	Selling	Sales	Cost %	Cost %	Margin	Margin	%
5		# Sold	(B6 / B16) %	Cost	(B6 x D6)	Price	(B6 x F6)	(D6 / F6) %	(E6 / G6) %	(F6-D6)	(G6-E6)	(K6 / K16) %
6	Minute steak	73	7.06%	4.83	352.59	14.95	1091.35	32.31%	32.31%	10.12	738.76	10.10%
7	Shrimp (Tiger)	121	11.70%	6.59	797.39	18.95	2292.95	34.78%	34.78%	12.36	1495.56	20.45%
8	Swordfish	105	10.15%	5.18	543.90	14.95	1569.75	34.65%	34.65%	9.77	1025.85	14.03%
9	Chicken	140	13.54%	2.14	299.60	7.25	1015.00	29.52%	29.52%	5.11	715.40	9.78%
10	Lobster	51	4.93%	8.64	440.64	21.00	1071.00	41.14%	41.14%	12.36	630.36	8.62%
11	Scallops	85	8.22%	3.39	288.15	9.95	845.75	34.07%	34.07%	6.56	557.60	7.62%
12	Beef medallions	125	12.09%	4.04	505.00	10.95	1368.75	36.89%	36.89%	6.91	863.75	11.81%
13	Pasta Primavera	155	14.99%	2.25	348.75	5.95	922.25	37.82%	37.82%	3.70	573.50	7.84%
14	Meatloaf	97	9.38%	2.75	266.75	6.95	674.15	39.57%	39.57%	4.20	407.40	5.57%
15	Potato Skin	82	7.93%	1.22	100.04	4.95	405.90	24.65%	24.65%	3.73	305.86	4.18%
16	Total:	1034	100.00%	41.03	3,942.81	115.85	11,256.85	XXXXXXX	XXXXXXX	74.82	7,314.04	100.00%
17	Averages:	103	10.00%	4.10	XXXXXXX	11.59	XXXXXXX	35.42%	35.03%	7.48	XXXXXXX	10.00%
18	Projected Cost Percentage:			35.42%								
19	Actual Cost Percentage:		minus	35.03%								
20		equals	Variance:	0.39%								
21	Highest Seller by # Sold:			155		Highest Seller $:		2292.95				
22	Lowest Seller by # Sold:			51		Lowest Seller $:		405.90		AVG Item CM $:		7.48
23			Best Cost %:	24.65%		Highest CM $:		1495.56		Highest Item CM $:		12.36
24			Worst Cost %:	41.14%		Lowest CM $:		305.86		Lowest Item CM $:		3.70

In the above illustration the best seller by numbers sold is: (155) the Pasta Primavera with a below average CM% and a above average Cost %

Best Seller by Revenue is: Tiger Shrimp ($2,292.85), the Cost % is below average and it has the highest CM%

SalesMix by Klaus Theyer C.C.C.

	MENU ITEMS: CATEGORY:	Cost of Product	Selling Price	Item Desired Cost %	Section Desired Cost %	Number of Items Sold	Sales Mix %	C.O.G.S.	Revenue Item or Category	Actual Cost % by Category
6	**Appetizer**									
7	1 Item #1	2.95	7.50	39.33%		4	16.67%	11.80	30.00	
8	2 Item #2	2.50	7.50	33.33%		8	33.33%	20.00	60.00	
9	3 Item #3	1.85	7.50	24.67%		12	50.00%	22.20	90.00	
10	SectionTotal:	7.30	22.50		32.44%	24	100%	54.00	180.00	30.00%
11	**Soup**									
12	4 Item #1	1.50	5.00	30.00%		20	44.44%	30.00	100.00	
13	5 Item #2	1.05	5.00	21.00%		15	33.33%	15.75	75.00	
14	6 Item #3	1.75	5.00	35.00%		10	22.22%	17.50	50.00	
15	SectionTotal:	4.30	15.00		28.67%	45	100%	63.25	225.00	28.11%
16	**Salads**									
17	7 Item #1	1.10	5.50	20.00%		5	27.78%	5.50	27.50	
18	8 Item #2	1.55	5.50	28.18%		8	44.44%	12.40	44.00	
19	9 Item #3	2.10	5.50	38.18%		5	27.78%	10.50	27.50	
20	SectionTotal:	4.75	16.50		28.79%	18	100%	28.40	99.00	28.69%
21	**Fish - Main-Courses**									
22	10 Item #1	5.75	17.50	32.86%		6	25.00%	34.50	105.00	
23	11 Item #2	4.80	17.50	27.43%		10	41.67%	48.00	175.00	
24	12 Item #3	5.25	17.50	30.00%		8	33.33%	42.00	140.00	
25	SectionTotal:	15.80	52.50		30.10%	24	100%	124.50	420.00	29.64%
26	**Veal**									
27	13 Item #1	4.95	18.50	26.76%		4	20.00%	19.80	74.00	
28	14 Item #2	5.75	18.50	31.08%		7	35.00%	40.25	129.50	
29	15 Item #3	6.85	18.50	37.03%		9	45.00%	61.65	166.50	
30	SectionTotal:	17.55	55.50		31.62%	20	100%	121.70	370.00	32.89%
31	**Poultry**									
32	16 Item #1	3.00	10.50	28.57%		12	28.57%	36.00	126.00	
33	17 Item #2	3.25	10.50	30.95%		14	33.33%	45.50	147.00	
34	18 Item #3	3.85	10.50	36.67%		16	38.10%	61.60	168.00	
35	SectionTotal:	10.10	31.50		32.06%	42	100%	143.10	441.00	32.45%
36	**Pasta**									
37	19 Item #1	2.25	9.50	23.68%		14	27.45%	31.50	133.00	
38	20 Item #2	2.75	9.50	28.95%		22	43.14%	60.50	209.00	
39	21 Item #3	3.25	9.50	34.21%		15	29.41%	48.75	142.50	
40	SectionTotal:	8.25	28.50		28.95%	51	100%	140.75	484.50	29.05%
41	**Specials**									
42	22 Special#1	3.75	14.50	25.86%		25	55.56%	93.75	362.50	
43	23 Special#2	4.50	14.50	31.03%		20	44.44%	90.00	290.00	
44	SectionTotal:	8.25	29.00		28.45%	45	100%	183.75	652.50	28.16%
45	**Desserts**									
46	24 Item #1	1.25	4.75	26.32%		18	16.07%	22.50	85.50	
47	25 Item #2	1.45	4.75	30.53%		22	19.64%	31.90	104.50	
48	26 Item #3	1.55	4.75	32.63%		26	23.21%	40.30	123.50	
49	27 Item #4	1.65	4.75	34.74%		24	21.43%	39.60	114.00	
50	28 Item #5	1.75	4.75	36.84%		22	19.64%	38.50	104.50	
51	SectionTotal:	7.65	23.75		32.21%	112	100%	172.80	532.00	32.48%
52										
53	**Grand Totals:**	83.95	274.75		30.56%	381		1,032.25	3,404.00	30.32%

Compare the group item to the group average and contemplate adjustments.

Another helpful tool is comparing forecast with actual results and analysing the difference (Variance). Variances can be Positive or Negative. Although positive variances are welcome, it is essential to verify that there were no mistakes made in the menu pricing (Overpriced) or in the cost calculation (error in recipe) and the recording/input of information.

Variances can be calculated for almost anything – Before planning any variance report it must be decide what construed essential knowledge to be focused on.

	A	B	C	D	E	F	G	H	I	J
1	Budget - Sales - Variance Report							by Klaus Theyer CCC		
2										
3		Opening	Popularity						Projected	
4		Inventory	Index %							
5		# of items	Sales Mix	Selling	Item	Projected	Projected		Gross	
6	Menu Item	prepared	Menu Mix	Price	Cost	Cost	Revenue	Cost %	Profit	
7	Appetizers	40		7.50	1.75					
8	Salads	30		5.50	1.25					
9	Main	60		19.95	5.95					
10	Dessert	40		5.50	1.75					
11	Coffee	60		5.50	0.25					
12	Tea	15		5.50	0.25					
13	Wine White	20		7.50	2.25					
14	Wine Red	40		7.50	2.25					
15	Beer Dom	10		3.25	1.01					
16	Beer Import	15		4.75	1.65					
17	Soft Drinks	10		1.75	0.20					
18	Summary:									
19										
20			Popularity							
21			Index %							
22		# of items	Sales Mix	Selling	Item				Gross	+/-
23	Menu Item	Sold	Menu Mix	Price	Cost	COGS	Revenue	Cost %	Profit	Variance
24	Appetizers	30	8.52%	7.50	1.75					
25	Salads	35	9.94%	5.50	1.25					
26	Main	72	20.45%	19.95	5.95					
27	Dessert	45	12.78%	5.50	1.75					
28	Coffee	50	14.20%	5.50	0.25					
29	Tea	20	5.68%	5.50	0.25					
30	Wine White	15	4.26%	7.50	2.25					
31	Wine Red	40	11.36%	7.50	2.25					
32	Beer Dom	15	4.26%	3.25	1.01					
33	Beer Import	10	2.84%	4.75	1.65					
34	Soft Drinks	20	5.68%	1.75	0.20					
35	Summary:									
36	Budget:		N/A							
37	Variance +/-		N/A							

Budget - Sales - Variance Report

by Klaus Theyer CCC

Menu Item	Opening Inventory # of items prepared	Popularity Index % Sales Mix Menu Mix	Selling Price	Item Cost	Projected Cost	Projected Revenue	Cost %	Projected Gross Profit
Appetizers	40	11.76%	7.50	1.75	70.00	300.00	23.33%	230.00
Salads	30	8.82%	5.50	1.25	37.50	165.00	22.73%	127.50
Main	60	17.65%	19.95	5.95	357.00	1197.00	29.82%	840.00
Dessert	40	11.76%	5.50	1.75	70.00	220.00	31.82%	150.00
Coffee	60	17.65%	5.50	0.25	15.00	330.00	4.55%	315.00
Tea	15	4.41%	5.50	0.25	3.75	82.50	4.55%	78.75
Wine White	20	5.88%	7.50	2.25	45.00	150.00	30.00%	105.00
Wine Red	40	11.76%	7.50	2.25	90.00	300.00	30.00%	210.00
Beer Dom	10	2.94%	3.25	1.01	10.10	32.50	31.08%	22.40
Beer Import	15	4.41%	4.75	1.65	24.75	71.25	34.74%	46.50
Soft Drinks	10	2.94%	1.75	0.20	2.00	17.50	11.43%	15.50
Summary:	340	100.00%	74.20	18.56	725.10	2,865.75	25.30%	2,140.65

Menu Item	# of items Sold	Popularity Index % Sales Mix Menu Mix	Selling Price	Item Cost	COGS	Revenue	Cost %	Gross Profit	+/- Variance
Appetizers	30	8.52%	7.50	1.75	52.50	225.00	23.33%	172.50	-57.50
Salads	35	9.94%	5.50	1.25	43.75	192.50	22.73%	148.75	21.25
Main	72	20.45%	19.95	5.95	428.40	1,436.40	29.82%	1,008.00	168.00
Dessert	45	12.78%	5.50	1.75	78.75	247.50	31.82%	168.75	18.75
Coffee	50	14.20%	5.50	0.25	12.50	275.00	4.55%	262.50	-52.50
Tea	20	5.68%	5.50	0.25	5.00	110.00	4.55%	105.00	26.25
Wine White	15	4.26%	7.50	2.25	33.75	112.50	30.00%	78.75	-26.25
Wine Red	40	11.36%	7.50	2.25	90.00	300.00	30.00%	210.00	0.00
Beer Dom	15	4.26%	3.25	1.01	15.15	48.75	31.08%	33.60	11.20
Beer Import	10	2.84%	4.75	1.65	16.50	47.50	34.74%	31.00	-15.50
Soft Drinks	20	5.68%	1.75	0.20	4.00	35.00	11.43%	31.00	15.50
Summary:	352	100.00%	74.20	18.56	780.30	3,030.15	25.75%	2,249.85	109.20
Budget:	340	N/A	74.20	18.56	725.10	2,865.75	25.30%	2,140.65	0.00
Variance +/-	12	N/A	0.00	0.00	55.20	164.40	0.45%	109.20	109.20

The information derived from the above Variance report can be interpreted in many different ways although it was intended to measure the variance of Projected and Actual Gross Profit. The Task on hand is to find out what is the cause of the variance; Sales Mix? Costing calculations (Standard Recipe)? Selling Price calculations? Or was the Projection inaccurate? No conclusive answers can be drawn from the available information.

Depreciation – Capital Cost Allowance and Canada Revenue Agency

The term depreciation refers to the **"Loss of value over time"** of an asset. The loss of value is calculated using prescribed "Rates" based on assigned "Classes" as defined by Canada Revenue Agency, (formerly known as Revenue Canada).

Businesses commonly apply the calculated value of the "loss of value over time" against income in order to reduce the taxable income. Depreciation is a FXC Fixed Cost since time cannot be stopped.

Canada Revenue Agency has many rules about depreciation and Capital Cost Allowance (which is the reduction of value of an asset calculated by using a prescribed rate expressed in a percentage) and most commonly the "Diminishing or Declining Balance Method".

The opposite of Depreciation is Appreciation. Appreciation happens when an asset increases its value over time.

Example of depreciation:

Common kitchen equipment (Class 8 – Rate 20% per annum)

Cost of acquisition without GST	2,000.00
First year rule (deduct 50% of cost)	- 1,000.00
Balance	1,000.00
Year one Capital Cost Allowance (based on 20% rate)	200.00
Balance	800.00
First year rule deduction added back to asset cost	1,000.00
Balance	1,800.00
Year two Capital Cost Allowance (based on 20% rate)	360.00
Balance	1,440.00
Year three Capital Cost Allowance (based on 20% rate)	288.00
Un-depreciated Capital Cost Balance	1,152.00

This method is repeated year after year until the equipment is replaced, traded in, sold or scrapped.

If traded in and or sold and replaced the trade in is deducted from the last Balance and the cost of the replacement equipment is added to the remaining value and the depreciation process continues as previously illustrated, however, without the "First year rule calculation".

If the equipment was sold and it was the only or last one in its class (Class 8) – and NOT replaced – a possible Capital gain or a Capital loss may has occurred.

A Capital gain would occur if the equipment was sold for MORE than the Un-depreciated Capital Cost and a Capital Loss would occur if the equipment was sold for LESS than the Un-depreciated Capital Cost.

The rules about Depreciation and Capital Cost Allowance are rather complex and often confusing and calculations should be performed by professionals. Canada Revenue Agency lists Classes from 1 to 44 with Sub-Classes and Special Rules with rates from 4% to 100% as well as Fast-Write-Off for Energy efficient and other Special equipment. The 2007 Preparing your income tax returns book by C.C.H. a Wolters Kluwer Business features 110 pages on Capital Cost in small print.

The following page features two Capital Cost Allowance examples, one based on the common Canadian Diminishing Balance Method, and one based on the popular American Straight Line Method.

Space for notes:

In the following example the "First-Year-Rule" was not taken in consideration.

Depreciation Capital Cost Allowance examples

Depreciation (Capital Cost Allowance) Methods and Examples

Depreciation is the allowable compensation for "Loss of Value" of depreciable goods and/or Items.
Depreciation is the opposite of "Appreciation", in which case the value is increasing. Examples of appreciation would be Art-work, some Alcoholic beverages, Antiques.

C.C.A. Capital Cost Allowance   U.C.C. Un-depreciated Capital Cost (B.o.Y & E.o.Y.)
Depreciation RATE and AMOUNT   ACCRUED Depreciation

The following two methods are prescribed and or acceptable to Revenue Canada (permission for one of them is required); Diminishing Balance and Straight Line Method:

Info needed for Diminishing Balance:

1. Cost of acquisition without GST., including PST
2. Cost of installation inc. PST., excluding GST
3. Allowable Rate (%) of depreciation

1.	3200.00
2.	430.00
3.	20.00%

Capital equipment cost:

(inc. installation & PST)		3630.00		
C.C.A.	20%	726.00	Year 1
	U.C.C.	2904.00	
C.C.A.	20%	580.80	Year 2
	U.C.C.	2323.20	
C.C.A.	20%	464.64	Year 3
	U.C.C.	1858.56	
C.C.A.	20%	371.71	Year 4
	U.C.C.	1486.85	
C.C.A.	20%	297.37	Year 5

Accrued depreciation: 2440.52

U.C.C. after 5 years   1189.48

Info needed for Straight Line:

1. Cost of acquisition without GST., including PST
2. Cost of installation inc. PST., excluding GST
3. Salvage Value at the end of Life expectancy
4. Life expectancy in years

1.	3200.00
2.	430.00
3.	230.00
4.	5

Capital equipment cost:

(inc. installation & PST)	3630.00	
minus S.V.	230.00	
= U.C.C.	3400.00	
C.C.A.	680.00	Year 1
	680.00	Year 2
	680.00	Year 3
	680.00	Year 4
	680.00	Year 5

Accrued depreciation: 3400.00

U.C.C. after 5 years   0.00

Page for Notes:

Templates and Workshops

More and expanded Templates can be found @ www.MenuForProfit.com

Quick Conversion Factors for Kitchen and Bar

based on ESBUnitconv Website   http://www.esbconsult.com/esbcalc

updated   01/04/2007

NOTE: Significance of conversions should be limited to 4 decimal places.

VOLUME (Imperial Liquid Fluid)

1 Imp ounces = 28.41 ml, 1 imp gallon = 4 quarts = 8 pints = 160 fl ounces, 1 gallon = 4.5456 liters

1 Imp fl ounce = 28.41 ml   times 1.0408375 = 1 US fl ounces = 29.57 ml

1 liters = 10 deciliters = 1000 milliliters = 35.195 Imp fl ounces

1 Us fl oz = (29.574 ml) minus 1 Imp fl oz (28.413 ml) = 1.161 ml, hence the US fl oz is 1.161 ml (4.088%) larger then the Imp fl oz

		for accurate conversion			Simple Recipe conversion
#'s of Units	Unit	times x	=	to	
1	teaspoon	3.625116000		milliliters	5
1	tablespoon	14.500464000		milliliters	15
1	Imp fl ounce	28.410000000		milliliters	28.4
1	8 oz cup	0.2272800000		liters	0.23
1	½ pints	0.284100000		liters	284
1	pints	0.568200000		liters	0.57
1	quarts	1.136400000		liters	1.14
1	gallons	4.545600000		liters	4.55
1	Imp fl ounces	0.960764769		US fl ounces	0.96

		for accurate conversion			Simple Recipe conversion
#'s of Units	Unit	times x	=	to	
1	teaspoon	0.1276000000		Imp ounces	0.13
1	tablespoon	0.5104000000		Imp ounces	0.5
1	milliliters	0.0351988736		Imp ounces	0.04
1	250 ml	0.0351988736		Imp ounces	8.80
1	liters	35.1988736360		Imp ounces	35.20
1	liters	1.7599436818		Imp pints	1.76
1	liters	0.8799718409		Imp quarts	0.88
1	liters	0.2199929602		Imp gallons	0.22
1	Imp fl ounces	28.4100000000		millilitres	28.4

VOLUME (US Liquid Fluid)

1 US ounces = 29.57 ml, 1 US gallon = 4 quarts = 8 pints = 128 fl ounces, 1 gallon = 3.785 liters

1 US fl ounce = 29.57 ml   times 1.0408375 = 1 Imp fl ounces = 28.41 ml

1 liters = 10 deciliters = 1000 milliliters = 33.818 US fl ounces

1 Us fl oz = (29.57 ml) minus 1 Imp fl oz (28.41 ml) = 1.16 ml, hence the US fl oz is 1.16 ml (4.083%) larger then the Imp fl oz

1 ounce = 2 tblsp of liquid, 4 oz = 1/2 cup, 8 oz = 1 cup, 3 tsp = 1 tblsp, 1 tblsp = 1/16 of a cup, 4 tblsp = 1/4 cup, 8 tblsp = 1/2 cup,

1/2 lbs (8 oz) of butter = 1 cup, 1 lbs of butter = 2 cups, 2 cups = 1 pint, 2 pint = 1 quart, 4 quarts = 1 gallon or 3.785 Litres

		for accurate conversion			Simple Recipe conversion
#'s of Units	Unit	times x	=	to	
1	teaspoon	4.928365563		milliliters	5
1	tablespoon	14.78509669		milliliters	15
1	US fl ounce	29.5701934		milliliters	29.6
1	8 oz cup US	0.2365615470		liters	0.24
1	½ pints	0.236656155		liters	0.24
1	US pints	0.4731223094		liters	0.47
1	US quarts	0.9462461880		liters	0.95
1	US gallons	3.784984752		liters	3.8
1	US fl ounces	1.0408375000		Imp fl ounces	1.04

		for accurate conversion			Simple Recipe conversion
#'s of Units	Unit	times x	=	to	
1 US	teaspoon	0.1666666667		US fl ounces	0.17
1 US	tablespoon	0.5000000000		US fl ounces	0.5
1	milliliters	0.0338178377		US fl ounces	0.034
1	250 ml	8.4544594250		US fl ounces	8.500
1	liters	33.8178376894		US fl ounces	33.82
1	liters	2.1136148556		US pints	2.11
1	liters	1.056807428		US quarts	1.06
1	liters	0.2642018569		US gallons	0.264
1	Imp fl ounces	0.960764769		US fl ounces	0.96

Quick Conversion Factors for Kitchen or Bar
based on ESBUnitconv Website   http://www.esbconsult.com/esbcalc   updated   01/04/2007   Page 2

NOTE: Significance of conversions should be limited to 4 decimal places.

Quick Bar measurments conversion

1 Imp oz Shot	=	28.41 ml
1 ¼ Imp oz Shot	=	35.513 ml
1 ½ Imp oz Shot	=	42.615 ml
1 btl (26 imp fl oz) =	738.66 ml	.73866 L
1 btl (40 Imp oz) =	1136.40 ml	1.14 L
1 btl (250 ml) =	8.799 Imp oz	8.454 US oz
1 btl (500 ml) =	17.599 Imp oz	16.909 US oz
1 btl (750 ml) =	26.399 Imp oz	25.363 US oz
1 btl (1 L) =	35.199 Imp oz	33.818 US oz
1 btl (1750 ml) =	61.598 Imp oz	59.181 US oz
1 btl (2 L) =	70.398 Imp oz	67.636 US oz

WEIGHT conversions

#'s of Units	Unit	times	=	to	Simple Recipe conversion
1	Ounces (oz)	28.34952312		Grams (gr)	28.35
1	Grams	0.035273962		Ounces	0.04
1	Pounds (lbs)	0.45359237040		Kilograms	0.454
1	Pounds (lbs)	453.5923704		Grams (gr)	454
1	Kilograms	2.2046226199		Pounds	2.205
1	Kilograms	35.27399619558		Ounces	35.3
1	Metric Tons	1.102311311		Tons	1.1
1	Tons	0.9071847399		Metric Tons	0.91

1 Kg = 100 Decagrams = 1000 Grams = 2.205 Lbs
1 Pound = 16 Ounces = 454 Grams = .454 Kilograms

LENGTH

#'s of Units	Unit	times	=	to
1	inches	25.40		millimeters
1	inches	2.54		centimeters
1	inches	0.0254		meters
1	foot	0.305		meters
1	yard	0.91		meters
1	mile (land)	1.61		kilometers
1	nautical mi	1.85		kilometers

#'s of Units	Unit	times	=	to
1	millimeters	0.04		inches
1	centimeters	0.394		inches
1	meters	39.37		inches
1	meters	3.281		feet
1	meters	1.094		yards
1	kilometers	0.6214		miles
1	kilometers	0.540		nautical mi

in = inches, ft = foot (feet), yd = yard, mi = mile
12 inches = 1 foot, 3 feet = 1 yard, 5280 feet = 1 mile, 1 mile = 1760 yards
mm = millimeter, cm = centemeter, m = meter, km = kilometer
1 cm = 10 mm, 1 m = 100 cm = 1000 mm

TEMPERATURE

	Fahrenheit	to Celcius		Fahrenheit	to Celcius
F to C (F - 32) ÷ 9 × 5	32	0		Body 98.3	36.8
C to F (C × 9 ÷ 5) + 32	-40	-40		Room 70	21.11
F to C (F - 32) ÷ 1.8	-28	-33.33		Absolute 0	-273.15
C to F (C × 1.8) + 32	-18	-27.78		-459.67	Absolute 0

Fahrenheit

Fahrenheit	to Celcius	Fahrenheit	to Celcius
500	260	350	176.66
450	232.22	300	148.88
400	204.44	250	121.11
375	190.55	212	100

Calculator Warm-Up by Klaus Theyer C.C.C.

	A	B	C	D	E	F	G	H	I
3				Desired	Sales		Actual		
4				Cost % or	Price		Sales		
5	Product	Cost of Food and or		Mark-up	based on	Projected	Price	Actual	Variance
6	**Cost**	Cost objective		Cost plus	C% or Multp.	Cost %	-- is --	Cost % is	PC - AC
7	4.20	Food Cost Objective		67.00%		XXXXXXX	7.50		
8	2.09	Food Cost Objective		23.00%		XXXXXXX	8.50		
9	8.00	Food Cost Objective		55.00%		XXXXXXX	10.00		
10	2.03	Food Cost Objective		33.00%		XXXXXXX	5.00		
11	3.11	Food Cost Objective		88.00%		XXXXXXX	7.50		
12	0.66	Food Cost Objective		43.00%		XXXXXXX	2.00		
13	2.09	Profit plus Cost		1.16			3.25		
14	2.44	Profit plus Cost		1.16			3.60		
15	0.66	Markup		23.00%			1.00		
16	0.75	Markup		25.00%			1.75		
17	0.85	Markup		33.00%			1.50		
18	0.90	Markup 6/10's = ? %					2.50		
19	0.90	Markup 5/8's = ? %					3.50		
20	1.05	Markup		50.00%			4.00		
21	1.00	Markup 4/4's = ? %					1.00		
22	30.73	XXXXXXXXXXXXXXXXXX	XXXXXXX		57.33	53.60%	62.60	49.09%	4.51%

```
Total Cost                              Sellingprice
------------- x 100 = Actual/Aver F.C.%   ------------- x 100 = Cost
Sellingprice                             F.C. (%)

Cost                                                    Numerator
---------- x 100 = Sellingprice     Fraction Markup = --------------- = % (#)
F.C. (%)                                                Denominator (%)


                    Cost
Fraction  Markup = --------------- x Numerator + Cost = Sellingprice
                   Denominator


                      Cost x (%)
Percentage Markup = --------------- + Cost = S. P.
                         100
```

Calculator Warm-Up by Klaus Theyer C.C.C.

Product Cost	Cost of Food and or Cost objective	Desired Cost % or Mark-up Cost plus	Sales Price based on C% or Multp.	Projected Cost %	Actual Sales Price -- is --	Actual Cost % is	Variance PC - AC
4.20	Food Cost Objective	67.00%	6.27	XXXXXXX	7.50	56.00%	11.00%
2.09	Food Cost Objective	23.00%	9.09	XXXXXXX	8.50	24.59%	-1.59%
8.00	Food Cost Objective	55.00%	14.55	XXXXXXX	10.00	80.00%	-25.00%
2.03	Food Cost Objective	33.00%	6.15	XXXXXXX	5.00	40.60%	-7.60%
3.11	Food Cost Objective	88.00%	3.53	XXXXXXX	7.50	41.47%	46.53%
0.66	Food Cost Objective	43.00%	1.53	XXXXXXX	2.00	33.00%	10.00%
2.09	Profit plus Cost	1.16	3.25	64.31%	3.25	64.31%	0.00%
2.44	Profit plus Cost	1.16	3.60	67.78%	3.60	67.78%	0.00%
0.66	Markup	23.00%	0.81	81.30%	1.00	66.00%	15.30%
0.75	Markup	25.00%	0.94	80.00%	1.75	42.86%	37.14%
0.85	Markup	33.00%	1.13	75.19%	1.50	56.67%	18.52%
0.90	Markup 6/10's = ? %	60.00%	1.44	62.50%	2.50	36.00%	26.50%
0.90	Markup 5/8's = ? %	62.50%	1.46	61.54%	3.50	25.71%	35.82%
1.05	Markup	50.00%	1.58	66.67%	4.00	26.25%	40.42%
1.00	Markup 4/4's = ? %	100.00%	2.00	50.00%	1.00	100.00%	-50.00%
30.73	XXXXXXXXXXXXXXXXXX	XXXXXXX	57.33	53.60%	62.60	49.09%	4.51%

```
Total Cost                                    Sellingprice
-------------- x 100 = Actual/Aver F.C.%      -------------- x 100 = Cost
Sellingprice                                  F.C. (%)


Cost                                                         Numerator
---------- x 100 = Sellingprice          Fraction Markup = ---------------- = % (#)
F.C. (%)                                                     Denominator (%)


                       Cost
Fraction   Markup = ---------------- x Numerator + Cost = Sellingprice
                    Denominator


                    Cost x (%)
Percentage Markup = ------------- + Cost = S. P.
                       100
```

Easy Workshop by Klaus Theyer C.C.C.

1. A Pie is divided into [8] portions. [5] portions are sold. What percentage % of the Pie is remaining?

2. One portion of this Apple Pie costs [0.60] cents to prepare. How much does it cost to make [12] Pies?

3. What percentage % of the cost of a whole Pie is represented by one slice ?

4. If you were to sell one slice for [2.75] what is the Food Cost percentage % ?

5. If the desired Food Cost percentage is [32.00%] what would the Selling Price have to be ?

6. If the Food Cost is [25] percent % and the Selling Price is [2.50] what is the Product Cost in ¢ ?

7. To make one Pie, [1] Kg of Apples is needed, after peeling and trimming there is only [75%] left of the purchase weight. What is the actual weight, of the peeled and cored Apples in grams ?

8. How many pounds (lbs) of A.P. Apples are needed if the recipe calls for [5] lbs of U.P. Apples.

9. If Apples average [8] oz each, how many Apples would you have to buy in the previous question?

10. If the Apples cost [1.21] per Kg, what is the total cost of the bought Apples in ounces

Sales mix - Menu mix - Popularity Index

Item Name	Sold	% of Sale		Item Name	Sold	% of Sale
11 Cheeseburger	14			19 Coffee Columbia	42	
12 Hamburger	18			20 Coffee Dark Roast	23	
13 Hot Dog	12			21 Coffee Decaffeinated	12	
14 Poutine	6			22 Coffee Arabica	18	
15 French Fries	36			23 Coke/Pepsi	26	
16 Chef Salad	10			24 Diet Coke/Pepsi	43	
17 Apple Pie portion	22			25 Milk 2% (1/2 pint)	14	
18 Ice Cream	11			26 Red Wine 5 oz glass	28	
Total				Total		

A Chef's Companion to Cost Control

Easy Workshop by Klaus Theyer C.C.C.

1. A Pie is divided into [8] portions. [5] portions are sold. What percentage % of the Pie is remaining? **37.50%**

2. One portion of this Apple Pie costs [0.60] cents to prepare. How much does it cost to make [12] Pies? **57.60**

3. What percentage % of the cost of a whole Pie is represented by one slice ? **12.50**

4. If you were to sell one slice for [2.75] what is the Food Cost percentage % ? **21.82%**

5. If the desired Food Cost percentage is [32.00%] what would the Selling Price have to be ? **1.875**

6. If the Food Cost is [25] percent % and the Selling Price is [2.50] what is the Product Cost in ¢ ? **62.5**

7. To make one Pie, [1] Kg of Apples is needed, after peeling and trimming there is only [75%] left of the purchase weight. What is the actual weight, of the peeled and cored Apples in grams ? **750** in ounces **26.455**

8. How many pounds (lbs) of A.P. Apples are needed if the recipe calls for [5] lbs of U.P. Apples. **6.667**

9. If Apples average [8] oz each, how many Apples would you have to buy in the previous question? **13.333**

10. If the Apples cost [1.21] per Kg, what is the total cost of the bought Apples **3.659**

Sales mix - Menu mix - Popularity Index

	Item Name	Sold	% of Sale		Item Name	Sold	% of Sale
11	Cheeseburger	14	10.85%	19	Coffee Columbia	42	20.39%
12	Hamburger	18	13.95%	20	Coffee Dark Roast	23	11.17%
13	Hot Dog	12	9.30%	21	Coffee Decaffeinated	12	5.83%
14	Poutine	6	4.65%	22	Coffee Arabica	18	8.74%
15	French Fries	36	27.91%	23	Coke/Pepsi	26	12.62%
16	Chef Salad	10	7.75%	24	Diet Coke/Pepsi	43	20.87%
17	Apple Pie portion	22	17.05%	25	Milk 2% (1/2 pint)	14	6.80%
18	Ice Cream	11	8.53%	26	Red Wine 5 oz glass	28	13.59%
	Total	129	100.00%		Total	206	100.00%

	A	B	C	D	E	F	G
1	Yield Test "A"		by Klaus Theyer C.C.C.				
2							
3	A.P. = As Purchased			E.P. = Edible Portion (Yield)			
4	A.P. - E.P. = Loss (Kg)			E.P. Weight / A.P. Weight = Yield %			
5	Loss Weight/ A.P. Weight = L %			U.P. = Usable Portion			
6							
7	**Calculate the Yield % and Loss % for each of the eight items.**						
8							
9	Item	Raw	Cooked	Yield %	Loss	Loss %	
10	A	6.170	4.900		1.270		
11							
12	B	6.100	4.800		1.300		
13							
14	C	6.200	4.950		1.250		
15							
16	D	6.150	4.850		1.300		
17							
18	Totals:						
19							
20	Averages:						
21	**Note: Yield and Loss percentages are based on total A.P. , E.P.,**						
22	**and total Loss**						
23	**For the example "A,B,C,D," the average weight A.P. in Kg is:**						
24				The average yield in Kg is:			
25				and the yield percentage is:			
26							
27	You are arranging a banquet for			390	Each person is to		
28	receive a	175		gr E.P. How many pieces do you have to get A.P. if			
29	each piece weighs		6.155	Kg A.P. (follow four steps below)			
30							
31	Step # 1	Multiply portion weight by customers (= Gr)					
32							
33	Step # 2	Total Cooked weight divided by 1000 = Kg					
34							
35	Step # 3	Divide Cooked weight by Yield % (x 100)					
36							
37	Step # 4	Divide Result (#3) weight by Raw weight A.P.					
38							

	A	B	C	D	E	F	G
1	Yield Test "A"		by Klaus Theyer C.C.C.				
2							
3	A.P. = As Purchased			E.P. = Edible Portion (Yield)			
4	A.P. - E.P. = Loss (Kg)			E.P. Weight / A.P. Weight = Yield %			
5	Loss Weight/ A.P. Weight = L %			U.P. = Usable Portion			
6							
7	**Calculate the Yield % and Loss % for each of the eight items.**						
8							
9		Item	Raw	Cooked	Yield %	Loss	Loss %
10		A	6.170	4.900	79.417%	1.270	20.583%
11							
12		B	6.100	4.800	78.689%	1.300	21.311%
13							
14		C	6.200	4.950	79.839%	1.250	20.161%
15							
16		D	6.150	4.850	78.862%	1.300	21.138%
17							
18	Totals:		24.620	19.500		5.120	
19							
20	Averages:		6.155	4.875	79.204%	1.280	20.796%
21	**Note: Yield and Loss percentages are based on total A.P. , E.P.,**						
22	**and total Loss**						
23	**For the example "A,B,C,D," the average weight A.P. in Kg is:**						6.155
24				The average yield in Kg is:			4.88
25				and the yield percentage is:			79.204%
26							
27	You are arranging a banquet for			390	Each person is to		
28	receive a		175	gr E.P. How many pieces do you have to get A.P. if			
29	each piece weighs			6.155	Kg A.P. (follow four steps below)		
30							
31	Step # 1	Multiply portion weight by customers (= Gr)				68250	
32							
33	Step # 2	Total Cooked weight divided by 1000 = Kg				68.25	
34							
35	Step # 3	Divide Cooked weight by Yield % (x 100)				86.17	
36							
37	Step # 4	Divide Result (#3) weight by Raw weight A.P.				14.00	
38							

	A	B	C	D	E	F	G	H	I	J	K	L	M	N	O	P
1	Bar INVENTORY	by Klaus Theyer C.C.C.													Purchasing:	
2	Bar Perpetual Inventory System:															
3				O.I. or Purcha. Date:	O.I. plus Quantity IN:			Invent. Date:					Inventory Extended Cost:			
4	Product from Bin Card:		Bottle Cont. ml						Quantity OUT:	Perpetual Inventory:	Actual Inventory:	Variance:		Par Stock:	Re-Order Quantity:	Cost of Re-Order:
5	Product Name:	Code:				Unit Cost:	Cost:									
6	Ballantine	3186	1136	01/01/07	6	32.40		01/01/07	4.5		2			3		
7	Chivas Regal 12Y old	68312	1750		4	62.25			3		1			2		
8	LCBO Extra Special	79418	1136		6	27.50			5		1			5		
9	34637 Canadian Club	34637	1750		5	44.50			3		2			4		
10	Seag. Crown Royal	10108	1136		3	32.40			1.75		1			2		
11	J.D. Sour Mash	89177	1136		2	30.60			1		1			2		
12	Alberta Pure Vodka	53082	1750		6	35.00			4		2			3		
13	McGuinness Red Tass	80648	1750		4	35.00			2		2			3		
14	Smirnoff Vodka	38505	1750		6	40.50			5		1			6		
15	Gilbey's Gin	67166	1750		6	39.90			4		2			4		
16	Gordon's Dry Gin	802	1136		3	27.00			1		2			4		
17	Shenley's Gin	56978	1750		2	39.90			2		1			2		
18	Bacardi Light Amber	85811	1750		6	40.90			4		2			4		
19	Captain Morgan Dark	150102	1136		6	28.05			5		1			6		
20	Marauder White	222695	1140		6	26.35			4		2			3		
21	Saint Remy	163519	1136		4	26.35			4		0			4		
22	DeVal. Napoleon VSOI	171876	1140		2	26.35			1.75		0			1		
23	Courvasier VS	1925	750		2	42.95			1		1			1		
24	Remy Martin VSOP	4101	750		2	60.35			1		1			1		
25	Hennessy VSOP	43703	750		2	69.50			1		1			1		
26	LCBO Import Brandy	118117	750		6	22.90			2		3			4		
27	Marqee De M. Armana	30981	750		4	24.00			3		1			2		
28	Calvados Boulard	38414	750		2	28.65			0.75		1			2		
29	Sauza SilvaTequila	17384	1140		6	26.35			5		1			2		
30	Peppermint Schnapps	183467	750		3	15.20			2		1			2		
31	Baileys Cream	74393	750		4	22.50			3		1			2		
32	Grand Marnier	1784	750		4	49.95			2		2			2		
33	Cointreau	6502	750		4	42.95			1		3			3		
34	Kahlua	79913	1750		6	49.20			5		1			3		
35	Tia Maria	398	750		6	24.50			4		1			3		
36	Drambuie	1867	750		6	42.95			3		3			4		
37	Amaretto Di Saronno	2253	750		3	22.50			2		1			2		
38	TOTALS:															

Bar INVENTORY

by Klaus Theyer C.C.C.

Bar Perpetual Inventory System:

Purchasing:

Product from Bin Card:		Bottle	O.I. or Purcha. Date:	O.I. plus Quantity IN:	Unit Cost:	Cost:	Invent. Date:	Quantity OUT:	Perpetual Inventory:	Actual Inventory:	Variance:	Inventory Extended Cost:	Par Stock:	Re-Order Quantity:	Cost of Re-Order:
Product Name:	Code:	Cont. ml													
Ballantine	3186	1136	01/01/07	6	32.40	194.40	01/01/07	4.5	1.5	2	0.5	64.80	3	1	32.40
Chivas Regal 12Y old	68312	1750		4	62.25	249.00		3	1	1	0	62.25	2	1	62.25
LCBO Extra Special	79418	1136		6	27.50	165.00		5	1	1	0	27.50	5	4	110.00
34637 Canadian Club	34637	1750		5	44.50	222.50		3	2	2	0	89.00	4	2	89.00
Seag. Crown Royal	10108	1136		3	32.40	97.20		1.75	1.25	1	-0.25	32.40	2	1	32.40
J.D. Sour Mash	89177	1136		2	30.60	61.20		1	1	1	0	30.60	2	1	30.60
Alberta Pure Vodka	53082	1750		6	35.00	210.00		4	2	2	0	70.00	3	1	35.00
McGuinness Red Tass	80648	1750		4	35.00	140.00		2	2	2	0	70.00	3	1	35.00
Smirnoff Vodka	38505	1750		6	40.50	243.00		5	1	1	0	40.50	6	5	202.50
Gilbey's Gin	67166	1750		6	39.90	239.40		4	2	2	0	79.80	4	2	79.80
Gordon's Dry Gin	802	1136		3	27.00	81.00		1	2	2	0	54.00	4	2	54.00
Shenley's Gin	56978	1750		2	39.90	79.80		2	0	1	1	39.90	2	1	39.90
Bacardi Light Amber	85811	1750		6	40.90	245.40		4	2	2	0	81.80	4	2	81.80
Captain Morgan Dark	150102	1136		6	28.05	168.30		5	1	1	0	28.05	6	5	140.25
Marauder White	222695	1140		6	26.35	158.10		4	2	2	0	52.70	3	1	26.35
Saint Remy	163519	1136		4	26.35	105.40		4	0	0	0	0.00	4	4	105.40
DeVal. Napoleon VSOI	171876	1140		2	26.35	52.70		1.75	0.25	0	-0.25	0.00	1	1	26.35
Courvasier VS	1925	750		2	42.95	85.90		1	1	1	0	42.95	1	0	0.00
Remy Martin VSOP	4101	750		2	60.35	120.70		1	1	1	0	60.35	1	0	0.00
Hennessy VSOP	43703	750		2	69.50	139.00		1	1	1	0	69.50	1	0	0.00
LCBO Import Brandy	118117	750		6	22.90	137.40		2	4	3	-1	68.70	4	1	22.90
Marqee De M. Armana	30981	750		4	24.00	96.00		3	1	1	0	24.00	2	1	24.00
Calvados Boulard	38414	750		2	28.65	57.30		0.75	1.25	1	-0.25	28.65	2	1	28.65
Sauza Silva Tequila	17384	1140		6	26.35	158.10		5	1	1	0	26.35	2	1	26.35
Peppermint Schnapps	183467	750		3	15.20	45.60		2	1	1	0	15.20	2	1	15.20
Baileys Cream	74393	750		4	22.50	90.00		3	1	1	0	22.50	2	1	22.50
Grand Marnier	1784	750		4	49.95	199.80		2	2	2	0	99.90	2	0	0.00
Cointreau	6502	750		4	42.95	171.80		1	3	3	0	128.85	3	0	0.00
Kahlua	79913	1750		6	49.20	295.20		5	1	1	0	49.20	3	2	98.40
Tia Maria	398	750		6	24.50	147.00		4	2	1	-1	24.50	3	2	49.00
Drambuie	1867	750		6	42.95	257.70		3	3	3	0	128.85	4	1	42.95
Amaretto Di Saronno	2253	750		3	22.50	67.50		2	1	1	0	22.50	2	1	22.50
TOTALS:				137	1,139.40	4,781.40		90.75	46.25	45	-1.25	1,635.30	92	47	1,535.45

	A	B	C	D	E	F	G	H	I	J	K	L	M
1	Bar One	Simple Menu Analysis Answers											
2	All drink names are from:		www.mixed-drink.com										
3			Popularity	Item	Total	Selling	Total	Project. Product Cost %	Actual Product Cost %	Item's Contrib. Margin	Total Contrib. Margin	G.P. Contrib. Margin %	Margin to Revenue %
4	Menu Item:	# Sold	Index	Cost	Cost	Price	Sales						
5	G-Red Cloud	73		1.30		6.50							
6	G-Typhoon	121		1.25		6.50							
7	G-Boomerang	105		1.20		6.50							
8	V-Sputnik	140		1.35		7.25							
9	V-Naked Pretzel	51		1.55		7.25							
10	V-Jungle Jane	85		1.45		7.25							
11	T-T-N-T	125		1.75		7.95							
12	T-Hot Pants	155		1.80		7.95							
13	T-Brave Bull	97		1.65		7.95							
14	R-Hop-Frog	68		1.30		6.95							
15	R-Casa Blanca	77		1.35		6.95							
16	R-Dingo Salad	82		1.40		6.95							
17	Total:												
18	Averages:												
19													
20	Projected Cost Percentage:												
21	Actual Cost Percentage:												
22	Variance:					Highest Seller $:				AVG Item CM $:			
23	Highest Seller by # Sold:					Lowest Seller $:				Highest Item CM $:			
24	Lowest Seller by # Sold:					Highest CM $:				Lowest Item CM $:			
25		Best Cost %:				Lowest CM $:							
26		Worst Cost %:											

	A	B	C	D	E	F	G	H	I	J	K	L	M
1	Bar One	Simple Menu Analysis Answers											
2	All drink names are from:	www.mixed-drink.com											
3			Popularity	Item	Total	Selling	Total	Project. Product Cost %	Actual Product Cost %	Item's Contrib. Margin	Total Contrib. Margin	G.P. Contrib. Margin %	Margin to Revenue %
4	Menu Item:	# Sold	Index	Cost	Cost	Price	Sales						
5	G-Red Cloud	73	6.19%	1.30	94.90	6.50	474.50	20.00%	20.00%	5.20	379.60	5.59%	4.46%
6	G-Typhoon	121	10.26%	1.25	151.25	6.50	786.50	19.23%	19.23%	5.25	635.25	9.35%	7.46%
7	G-Boomerang	105	8.91%	1.20	126.00	6.50	682.50	18.46%	18.46%	5.30	556.50	8.19%	6.53%
8	V-Sputnik	140	11.87%	1.35	189.00	7.25	1015.00	18.62%	18.62%	5.90	826.00	12.16%	9.70%
9	V-Naked Pretzel	51	4.33%	1.55	79.05	7.25	369.75	21.38%	21.38%	5.70	290.70	4.28%	3.41%
10	V-Jungle Jane	85	7.21%	1.45	123.25	7.25	616.25	20.00%	20.00%	5.80	493.00	7.26%	5.79%
11	T-T-N-T	125	10.60%	1.75	218.75	7.95	993.75	22.01%	22.01%	6.20	775.00	11.41%	9.10%
12	T-Hot Pants	155	13.15%	1.80	279.00	7.95	1232.25	22.64%	22.64%	6.15	953.25	14.04%	11.19%
13	T-Brave Bull	97	8.23%	1.65	160.05	7.95	771.15	20.75%	20.75%	6.30	611.10	9.00%	7.17%
14	R-Hop-Frog	68	5.77%	1.30	88.40	6.95	472.60	18.71%	18.71%	5.65	384.20	5.66%	4.51%
15	R-Casa Blanca	77	6.53%	1.35	103.95	6.95	535.15	19.42%	19.42%	5.60	431.20	6.35%	5.06%
16	R-Dingo Salad	82	6.96%	1.40	114.80	6.95	569.90	20.14%	20.14%	5.55	455.10	6.70%	5.34%
17	Total:	1179	100.00%	17.35	1,728.40	85.95	8,519.30	XXXXXX	XXXXXX	68.60	6,790.90	100.00%	79.71%
18	Averages:	98	8.33%	1.45	XXXXXX	7.16	XXXXXX	20.19%	20.29%	5.72	XXXXXX	8.33%	6.64%
19													
20	Projected Cost Percentage:		20.19%										
21	Actual Cost Percentage:		20.29%										
22	Variance:		-0.10%			Highest Seller $:	1232.25			AVG Item CM $:	5.72		
23	Highest Seller by # Sold:		155			Lowest Seller $:	369.75			Highest Item CM $:	6.30		
24	Lowest Seller by # Sold:		51			Highest CM $:	953.25			Lowest Item CM $:	5.20		
25	Best Cost %:		18.46%			Lowest CM $:	290.70						
26	Worst Cost %:		22.64%										

Turkey Yield by Klaus Theyer C.C.C.

Keep all calculations at THREE decimal places

Part one

Based on the following information, answer the accompanying questions:

Show the formulas used to calculate the result.

Turkey

	AP	Cost	$ 5.80	per Kg
		Weight	6.25	Kg
	UP	Weight	5.50	Kg

The percentage Yield for the cooked (U.P.) Turkey is ?

After carving there are **2.7** Kg Bones left

What is the edible (E.P.) weight in Kg?

The percentage Yield for the cooked (E.P.) Turkey is ?

The cost of one E.P. cooked Kg is?

What is the cost of a **150** Gr portion is ?

Side dishes (Line Cost) is **$ 1.75**

Total cost of one Turkey meal ?

Part two

You are contemplating different Selling Price scenarios by using the most common method; Cost divided by Cost % = S.P.

Potential Selling Price based on listed Cost Percentages:

24.00%	26.00%	28.00%	30.00%	32.00%	34.00%

The Menu Price is: **$ 12.95**   Actual Cost % is ?

Part three

Based on the result of **Part one**, how many raw (A.P.) Turkeys would you have to buy to serve **410** Customers ?

Step one: # of Customers X portion size in Grams:

Step two: Divide result by 1000 to convert to Kg:

Step three: Divide Kg by Yield %:

Step four: Divide A.P. Kg by weight of one Turkey.

How much is the A.P. cost to serve the 410 Customers ?

Turkey Yield by Klaus Theyer C.C.C.

Keep all calculations at THREE decimal places

Part one

Based on the following information, answer the accompanying questions:

Show the formulas used to calculate the result

Turkey			
AP	Cost	$ 5.80	per Kg
	Weight	6.25	Kg
UP	Weight	5.50	Kg

The percentage Yield for the cooked (U.P.) Turkey is ? **88.00%**

After carving there are **2.7** Kg Bones left.

What is the edible (E.P.) weight in Kg ? **2.8**

The percentage Yield for the cooked (E.P.) Turkey is ? **44.80%**

The cost of one E.P. cooked Kg is? **$ 12.95**   **$ 1.942**

What is the cost of a **150** Gr portion is ?

Side dishes (Line Cost) is **$ 1.75**

Total cost of one Turkey meal ? **$ 3.69**

Part two

You are contemplating different Selling Price scenarios by using the most common method; Cost divided by Cost % = **S.P.**

Potential Selling Price based on listed Cost Percentages:

24.00%	26.00%	28.00%	30.00%	32.00%	34.00%
$ 15.38	$ 14.20	$ 13.19	$ 12.31	$ 11.54	$ 10.86

The Menu Price is: **$ 12.95**   Actual Cost % is ? **28.51%**

Part three

Based on the result of **Part one**, how many raw (**A.P.**) Turkeys would you have to buy to serve **410** Customers ?

Step one: # of Customers **X** portion size in Grams: **61500**

Step two: Divide result by 1000 to convert to Kg. **61.5**

Step three: Divide Kg by Yield %. **137.28**

Step four: Divide A.P. Kg by weight of one Turkey. **21.96**

How much is the **A.P.** cost to serve the 410 Customers ? **$ 796.21**

	A	B	C	D	E	F	G	H	I	J	K	L	M	N
1	Standard Recipe COSTING Form											Page # of #'s:		1 of 1
2	Recipe Name:	Singapore Sling												
3	Date: 01/01/07	Service location:		Cozy Bar				Recipe Category:		Gin Drinks			Recipe #:	1
4	Recipe Source/Reference:			Internet				Production time in minutes =>		5		Average Labour Hour Cost $		15.00
5	Portion Size/Weight/Volume described =>			1 Drink 6 to 8 ounces								Direct Labour Requirements:		
6	Yield Portions # ==>		1									Calculated labour cost:		1.25
7				A.P.	A.P.	A.P. Package content		A.P.	Yield %	Yield	Recipe	Recipe	Recipe	Extended
8				Package	Package	Weight or Volume		Cost $	(if needed)	adjusted	Unit	Units	Units	Recipe
9	Product/Ingredient specified:			i.e. Pieces	content	Converted to Recipe Units #				Cost	Cost	used in	in weight	Cost
10	(detailed product description)			Bag, Case	# of Units	Unit #	Weight/Volu.	$	%	$	$	#	volume/size	$
11	Cherry Brandy Bols LCBO 24380			Btl	750 Ml	25.5	US Fl Oz	19.10	90%	21.22	0.8322	0.5	US Fl Oz	0.416
12	Grenadine Syrup			Btl	1000 Ml	34	US Fl Oz	6.75	90%	7.50	0.2206	0.5	US Fl Oz	0.110
13	Gin, Gordons LCBO 802			Btl	1140 Ml	38.76	US Fl Oz	32.75	90%	36.39	0.9388	1	US Fl Oz	0.939
14	Sweet and Sour Mix (939 Gr = 4L)			1 Bg=939 Gr	4000 Ml	136	US Fl Oz	3.75	90%	4.17	0.0306	2	US Fl Oz	0.061
15	Carbonated water as needed			0	0	0	US Fl Oz	0.00	100%	0.00	0.0000	4	US Fl Oz	0.000
16	Maraschino Cherry Jar =2.5 L =120 Pc			Jar/120 Pc	120 Pc	120	piece	14.00	90%	15.56	0.1296	1	piece	0.130
17	6			0	0	0	0	0.00	100%	0.00	0.0000	0	0	0.000
18	7			0	0	0	0	0.00	100%	0.00	0.0000	0	0	0.000
19	8			0	0	0	0	0.00	100%	0.00	0.0000	0	0	0.000
20	9			0	0	0	0	0.00	100%	0.00	0.0000	0	0	0.000
21	10			0	0	0	0	0.00	100%	0.00	0.0000	0	0	0.000
22	11			0	0	0	0	0.00	100%	0.00	0.0000	0	0	0.000
23	12			0	0	0	0	0.00	100%	0.00	0.0000	0	0	0.000
24	13			0	0	0	0	0.00	100%	0.00	0.0000	0	0	0.000
25												Sub-Total:		1.656
26	Additional Recipe(s) used:							Over-production, Spice, Ice, Waste allowance in %. Input # of % =>					10%	0.166
27	0			0	0	0	0	0.00	100%	0	0	0	0	0
28	0			0	0	0	0	0.00	100%	0	0	0	0	0
29												Total Recipe Cost:		1.82
30										Div. by Yield Portions, Insert # from above:				1
31												Portion Cost:		1.82
32	S.P. calculated @ a Cost % of:			Additional Selling Price calculation scenarios:	C % calculated @ a S.P. of:					Input desired S.P. Selling Price ==>				7.50
33	C %:	= S.P. $	= G.P. $		S.P. $:	= C %	= G.P. $					G.P. Gross Profit:		5.68
34	20.00%	9.11	7.29		7.50	24.29%	5.68					Portion Cost %:		24.29%
35	30.00%	6.07	4.25		8.50	21.43%	6.68			Total Recipe Cost including Labour Cost				3.07
36	40.00%	4.55	2.73		9.50	19.18%	7.68					Portion Cost inc. Labour Cost:		3.07
37	50.00%	3.64	1.82		9.75	18.68%	7.93							
	Recipe updated by:		Klaus Theyer CCC							S.P. based on a	40%		Prime Cost % ==>	7.68

Recipe form designed by Klaus Theyer CCC

	A	B	C	D	E	F	G	H	I	J	K	L
1	Simple Menu Analysis		Sales		COGS	Menu	Revenue	Recipe or Project.	Actual	Item	Total	Contrib.
2	by Klaus Theyer C.C.C.		Menu Mix		Total	Price	Total	Product	Product	GP or CM	Sold Item	Margin
3			Popularity	Item	Cost	Selling	Sales	Cost %	Cost %	Contrib. Margin	Contrib. Margin	%
4	Menu Item:		Index %									
5		# Sold	(B6 / B16) %	Cost	(B6 x D6)	Price	(B6 x F6)	(D6 / F6) %	(E6 / G6) %	(F6-D6)	(G6-E6)	(K6 / K16) %
6	Minute steak	73		4.83		14.95						
7	Shrimp (Tiger)	121		6.59		18.95						
8	Swordfish	105		5.18		14.95						
9	Chicken	140		2.14		7.25						
10	Lobster	51		8.64		21.00						
11	Scallops	85		3.39		9.95						
12	Beef medallions	125		4.04		10.95						
13	Pasta Primavera	155		2.25		5.95						
14	Meatloaf	97		2.75		6.95						
15	Potato Skin	82		1.22		4.95						
16	Total:											
17	Averages:				XXXXXXX		XXXXXXX	XXXXXXX	XXXXXXX		XXXXXXX	
18	Projected Cost Percentage:											
19	Actual Cost Percentage: minus Variance:											
20	equals											
21	Highest Seller by # Sold:					Highest Seller $:				AVG Item CM $:		
22	Lowest Seller by # Sold:					Lowest Seller $:						
23	Best Cost %:					Highest CM $:				Highest Item CM $:		
24	Worst Cost %:					Lowest CM $:				Lowest Item CM $:		

A Chef's Companion to Cost Control

	A	B	C	D	E	F	G	H	I	J	K	L	M	N
1	Standard Recipe COSTING Form						NOTE: YELLOW HIGHLIGHTED AREAS ARE REQUIRED INPUT AREAS					Page # of # 's:		1 of
2	Recipe Name:	Vichyssoise												
3	Date:	0	Service location:		if applicable		Recipe Category:		Optional				Recipe #:	0
4	Recipe Source/Reference:			Identify Source of Recipe (i.e. On Cooking page 862)				Production time in minutes ##		30		Direct Labour Requirements:		
5	Portion Size/Weight/Volume described =>			20 x 200 ml portions							Average Labour Hour Cost $			16.00
6	Yield Portions # ==>		20	Recipe Units Described				All Recipe Units used SHOULD be stated in METRIC			Calculated labour cost:			8.00
7				A.P. Package i.e. Pieces	A.P. Package content # of Units	A.P. Package content Weight or Volume Converted to Recipe Units #	Weight/Volu.	A.P. Cost $	Yield % (if needed)	Yield adjusted Cost	Recipe Unit Cost	Recipe Units used in	Recipe Units in weight	Extended Recipe Cost
8														
9	Product/Ingredient specified:													
10	(detailed product description)					Unit #		$	%	$	$	#	volume/size	$
11	Leek, white part only (1 leek = 1 lbs)			cs	12.00	12.00	lbs	28.50	60%	47.50	3.958	2	lbs	7.917
12	Butter, unsalted, whole			cs	20 x 1 lbs	320.00	oz	51.90	100%	51.90	0.162	8	oz	1.298
13	Potato, P.E.I. Large dice			Bag, Case	40 kg	88.20	lbs	23.50	90%	26.11	0.296	2	lbs	0.592
14	Heavy Cream, 35%			botl	1 ltr	1000.00	ml	4.95	100%	4.95	0.005	700	ml	3.465
15	Chives			open	1 bunch	1.00	bunch	0.90	90%	1.00	1.000	1	bunch	1.000
16	Salt			Bag, Case	40 kg	0.00	TT	0.00	100%	0.00	0.000	0	TT	0.000
17	Pepper, ground, white			Bag, Case	1 kg	68.97	TblSp	6.90	100%	6.90	0.100	5	TblSp	0.500
18	8			0.00	0.00	0.00	0	0.00	100%	0.00	0.000	0	0	0.000
19	9			0.00	0.00	0.00	0	0.00	100%	0.00	0.000	0	0	0.000
20	10			0.00	0.00	0.00	0	0.00	100%	0.00	0.000	0	0	0.000
21	11			0.00	0.00	0.00	0	0.00	100%	0.00	0.000	0	0	0.000
22	12			0.00	0.00	0.00	0	0.00	100%	0.00	0.000	0	0	0.000
23	13			0.00	0.00	0.00	0	0.00	100%	0.00	0.000	0	0	0.000
24	14			0.00	0.00	0.00	0	0.00	100%	0.00	0.000	0	0	0.000
25	15			0.00	0.00	0.00	0	0.00	100%	0.00	0.000	0	0	0.000
26	16			0.00	0.00	0.00	0	0.00	100%	0.00	0.000	0	0	0.000
27	17			0.00	0.00	0.00	0	0.00	100%	0.00	0.000	0	0	0.000
28	18			0.00	0.00	0.00	0	0.00	100%	0.00	0.000	0	0	0.000
29	19			0.00	0.00	0.00	0	0.00	100%	0.00	0.000	0	0	0.000
30	20			0.00	0.00	0.00	0	0.00	100%	0.00	0.000	0	0	0.000
31	21			0.00	0.00	0.00	0	0.00	100%	0.00	0.000	0	0	0.000
32	Recipe form designed/updated 2006 by Klaus Theyer C.C.C.												Sub-Total:	14.772
33	Additional Recipe(s) used:							Over-production, Spice, Ice, Waste allowance in %. Input # of % =>					10%	1.477
34	Chicken Stock			pail	5 ltr	5.00	ltr	6.25	100%	6.25	1.250	3.5	ltr	4.375
35	2			0.00	0.00	0.00	0	0.00	100%	0.00	0.000	0	0	0.000
36	3			0.00	0.00	0.00	0	0.00	100%	0.00	0.000	0	0	0.000
37				Additional Selling Price calculation scenarios:							Total Recipe Cost:			20.62
38											Div. by Yield Portions, Insert # from above:			20
39	S.P. calculated @ a Cost % of:			C % calculated @ a S.P. of:							Portion Cost:			1.03
40	C %:	= S.P. $	= G.P. $	S.P. $:	= C %	= G.P. $					Input desired S.P. Selling Price ==>			5.00
41	15.00%	6.87	5.84	2.50	41.25%	1.47					G.P. Gross Profit:			3.97
42	20.00%	5.16	4.12	3.50	29.46%	2.47					Portion Cost %:			20.62%
43	25.00%	4.12	3.09	4.50	22.92%	3.47					Total Recipe Cost including Labour Cost			28.62
44	30.00%	3.44	2.41	5.50	18.75%	4.47					Portion Cost inc. Labour Cost			1.43
45	Recipe updated by:		Enter Your Name		32.00%	3.22	2.19	6.50	15.86%	5.47	Selling Price based on desired Prime Cost %, Insert percentage here ==>		45%	3.18

A Chef's Companion to Cost Control

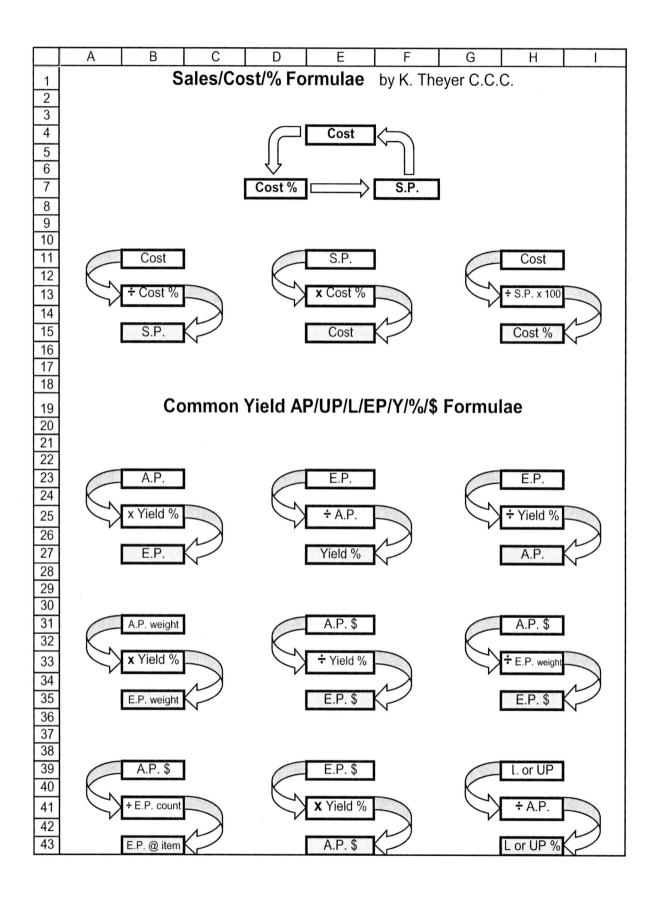

The Percentage Pie
by Klaus Theyer C.C.C.

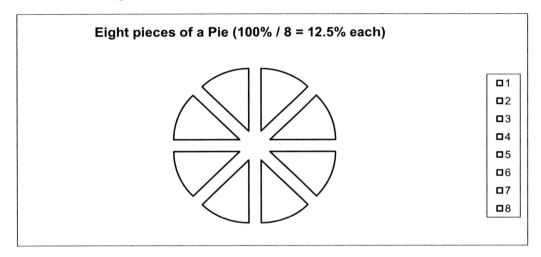

If one eight of a pie is 12.5%, how many percent is one twelfth?

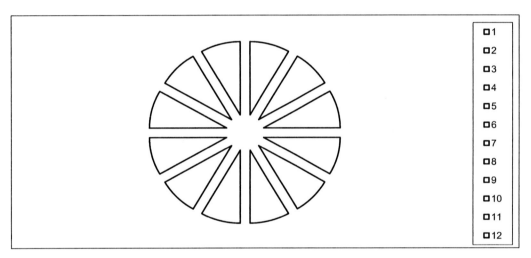

If one twelfth of a pie is 8.333%, how many percent is one sixteenth?

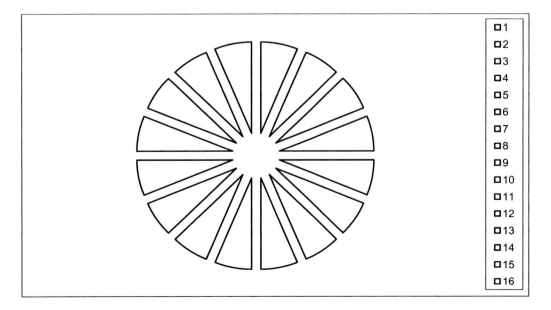

	A	B
1	From ONE dollar to a GOOGOLPLEX	
2	in US. Dollars,	as per Mr. Beakman, transcribed by Klaus Theyer C.C.C.
3	One	1
4	Ten	10
5	Hundred	100
6	Thousand	1,000
7	Million	1,000,000
8	Billion	1,000,000,000
9	Trillion	1,000,000,000,000
10	Quadrillion	1,000,000,000,000,000
11	Quintillion	1,000,000,000,000,000,000
12	Sextillion	1,000,000,000,000,000,000,000
13	Septillion	1,000,000,000,000,000,000,000,000
14	Octillion	1,000,000,000,000,000,000,000,000,000
15	Nonillion	1,000,000,000,000,000,000,000,000,000,000
16	Decillion	1,000,000,000,000,000,000,000,000,000,000,000
17	Undecillion	1,000,000,000,000,000,000,000,000,000,000,000,000
18	Duodecillion	1,000,000,000,000,000,000,000,000,000,000,000,000,000
19	Tredecillion	1,000,000,000,000,000,000,000,000,000,000,000,000,000,000
20	Quattuordecillion	1,000,000,000,000,000,000,000,000,000,000,000,000,000,000,000
21	Quindecillion	1,000,000,000,000,000,000,000,000,000,000,000,000,000,000,000,000
22	Sexdecillion	1,000,000,000,000,000,000,000,000,000,000,000,000,000,000,000,000,000
23	Septendecillion	1,000,000,000,000,000,000,000,000,000,000,000,000,000,000,000,000,000,000
24	Octodecillion	1,000,000,000,000,000,000,000,000,000,000,000,000,000,000,000,000,000,000,000
25	Novemdecillion	1,000,000,000,000,000,000,000,000,000,000,000,000,000,000,000,000,000,000,000,000
26	Vigintillion	1,000,000,000,000,000,000,000,000,000,000,000,000,000,000,000,000,000,000,000,000,000
27		
28	Googol	is a 1 with 100 Zeros behind
29	Googolplex	is a 1 with a googol of Zeros behind
30		
31	Usually, for numbers beyond a Trillion the Zeros are omitted - e.g. 1 Vigintillion = 10^{63}.	
32		
33		There is no such "thing" as a Zillion, it is a figure of speech
34		
35		If counted to a billion, counting one number per second, it would take you
36		31 years, 259 days, one houe, 46 minutes and 40 seconds
37		
38	As mentioned above, this scenario is based on US - Canadian Dollars - Europeans use a different system.	

Once your annual salary has reached a "Trillion" may consider retirement and sell this book. You may also make a donation to the Authors Retirement Fund – Good Luck.